Your Calling
as a Teacher

SEE ALSO

Your Calling as an Elder
Gary Straub

Your Calling as a Deacon
Gary Straub and James Trader II

Your Calling as a Leader
Gary Straub and Judy G. Turner

Your Calling as a Christian
Timothy L. Carson

Available at www.chalicepress.com

Your Calling
as a Teacher

Karen B. Tye

CHALICE
PRESS
ST. LOUIS, MISSOURI

Biblical quotations, unless otherwise noted, are from the *New Revised Standard Version Bible,* copyright 1989, Division of Christian Education of the National Council of the Churches of Christ in the United States of America. Used by permission. All rights reserved.

Those quotations marked RSV are from the *Revised Standard Version of the Bible,* copyright 1952, [2nd edition, 1971] by the Division of Christian Education of the National Council of the Churches of Christ in the United States of America. Used by permission. All rights reserved.

Cover and interior design: Elizabeth Wright

Visit Chalice Press on the World Wide Web at
www.chalicepress.com

10 9 8 7 6 5 4 3 2 1   08 09 10 11 12

Library of Congress Cataloging–in–Publication Data

Tye, Karen B.
  Your calling as a teacher / by Karen B. Tye.
    p. cm.
  ISBN 978-0-8272-4414-6
  1. Teaching–Religious aspects–Christianity. 2. Christian teachers–Religious life. I. Title.

  BV4596.T43T94 2008
  268'.3–dc22

                                                            2007050021

Printed in the United States of America

Contents

Introduction

The invitation comes in many ways. It may have been a phone call at home. Maybe the chair of the Christian education committee stopped you in the hall at church. Perhaps you found yourself checking the box beside "Sunday school teacher" on the "Time and Talent" sheet that was distributed as a part of the stewardship promotion in your church. Maybe the pastor made a plea from the pulpit about the need for teachers and you couldn't say no. Or you may be that pastor who accepted the responsibility to teach when you took your ordination vows. However the invitation came, you've agreed to be a teacher in the church. Whether you come willingly or because of a lot of nudging, whether you approach the task with great trepidation or with a sense of excitement and anticipation, however you come, you have said yes to the call to teach.

To most of us, teaching in the church is an awesome and daunting task. We are being asked to help shape and form children, youth, and adults in their Christian identity. We wonder if we are up to the task. Like people of faith of old, we can certainly think of all the excuses why we can't do this: I'm too young (Jeremiah); I'm not good enough (Isaiah); I can't stand up in front of a group and talk (Moses); I've got too many other things to do (Martha). In spite of our hesitation and our questions, however, we have answered the call and said yes. The question comes: Now what?

This book is written to help you answer the "Now what?" Its purpose is fourfold. First, it is designed to help you see and understand your teaching as a calling and a ministry, not just another job you are doing for the church. Second, it seeks to reflect with you on who and what a teacher is, dispelling some of the myths and misperceptions you have about teachers and teaching. Third, it provides information regarding good teaching practices, looking at some of the knowledge, skills, and tools that can help you faithfully carry out the ministry you are undertaking. And, finally, it celebrates with you all those who are called to teach in the community of faith. At the end of each chapter, some questions and opportunities invite you to further reflection on what you have just read.

This book is designed for those who teach in various capacities within the community of faith. Whether one is a Sunday school teacher, a nursery volunteer, a youth group advisor, the leader of an adult Bible study group, a vacation Bible school teacher, or a pastor, you are a teacher. The call you have accepted is a vital one. As a teacher, you are called to help equip the saints for ministry and to build up the body of Christ. This is an absolutely essential ministry of the church.

None of us would be where we are on our faith journeys without the teachers in our lives. Whether we were born and raised in the church or came to it at a later point, teachers helped us on the way. I see some of them in my mind's eye. There is Mrs. H.–a warm, friendly, grandmotherly figure that greeted me every Sunday when my parents left me at the door of the preschool room at First Christian Church, Richmond, Indiana. There is Mrs. K.–a quiet, gentle woman who led a group of pre-adolescent girls across the threshold into their teenage years and helped them learn in those Junior High Sunday school class sessions something about what it means to be a disciple of Jesus Christ. There is E.W.–a summer camp counselor who took time to listen to a young teenager struggling with all the changes that come during that stage of life. There is Rev. B.–an associate pastor who challenged a boisterous and energetic CYF group to think about hard and difficult questions and helped them find some answers. There is Mr. D., who faithfully prepares the weekly lesson for his senior adult class, always looking for ways to engage them and bring new insight about the gospel that will guide them in their final years. Such a great cloud of witnesses, these teachers who guide and teach us! They are the quiet saints who faithfully nurture us in our Christian faith.

God calls you to join this cloud of witnesses. You may have doubts and wonder if you can do it. But you can rest assured that you do not answer your call alone. Like those saints of old, you are surrounded, embraced, and upheld by the Spirit that calls us all. With the Spirit's help, it is my hope that in the pages ahead you will find insight and information that will dispel some of your doubts and worries and equip you with energy and enthusiasm for the ministry of teaching you have been called to do. Let the journey begin!

PART ONE

Called to Be a Teacher

> "Hear, O Israel: The LORD our God is one LORD; and you
> shall love the Lord your God with all your heart, and with all
> your soul, and with all your might. And these words which
> I command you this day shall be upon your heart; and you
> shall teach them diligently to your children, and shall talk
> of them when you sit in your house, and when you walk
> by the way, and when you lie down, and when you rise."
> (Deut. 6:4–7, RSV)

It is obvious that from the earliest days our ancient Hebrew ancestors saw teaching as a central task of the household of faith. But what defines teaching? How are we to understand this important work? Too often when we think about teaching in the church, we start with how to do it. While it is certainly important to think about how we teach, it is also vital that we think about what teaching is. Certainly, what we think it is will shape how we do it!

The title of this book, *Your Calling as a Teacher,* already suggests an understanding of what teaching is. It is a calling. What does it mean to say teaching is a calling? What is the relationship between calling and ministry? How might these perspectives on teaching shape our work as teachers?

Not only do we need to think about what teaching is, but we also need to think about who a teacher is. If we claim that teaching is a calling and ministry, what does this say about the teacher, who he is and what she does? What does it mean to be called a teacher in the context of the church?

In part one of this book, we explore both of these questions. In chapter 1 we look at the ministry of teaching, exploring what it means to be called to such a ministry. In chapter 2 we consider who a teacher is, reflecting on the qualities and roles that define a teacher in the church.

The Ministry of Teaching

Now you are the body of Christ and individually members of it. And God has appointed in the church first apostles, second prophets, third teachers; then deeds of power, then gifts of healing, forms of assistance, forms of leadership, various kinds of tongues. (1 Cor. 12:27–28)

You've said yes! As the reality sinks in, you begin to wonder—what have I done? How could I possibly have thought I could do this? I can't be a teacher. I don't know enough, this is too awesome a task, and I don't have anything to offer these children (or youth, or adults). What was I thinking?

Let me invite you to ponder with me this calling as a teacher. You are right—it is an awesome task! It is an important and vital ministry in the community of faith. This has been true throughout the history of the Christian movement. One of the most important titles given to Jesus was that of teacher. The gospels refer to him forty-eight times as *didaskalos,* or teacher. However, the call to teach did not stop with him. Jesus called the disciples and sent them out to teach and proclaim the good news. Also, the apostle Paul regularly talked about teaching as a vital gift in the early church's life.

Why is teaching so central to the church's life? For me, one of the earliest stories told about the church's beginnings reveals the answer to this question. In this story, a newly appointed leader of the church, Philip, encounters an Ethiopian eunuch on the road between Jerusalem and Gaza. As told in Acts 8:26–40, Philip comes upon the eunuch reading the prophet Isaiah and asks him if he understands what he is reading. The eunuch's reply, "How can I, unless someone guides me?" clearly expresses the reason why the church needs those who teach. How can any of us understand what it means to be a Christian and to follow Christ unless someone guides and nurtures us in our faith and belief? Your call to teach is a call to step out in faith as a guide for those who seek to know and understand.

Okay, you say, you can see that this is vital and important work in the church. We won't have a future as a church if we are not guiding and nurturing each new generation. But what about these terms, *calling* and *ministry*? What do we mean when we affirm that teaching is a calling and a ministry in the church? Aren't pastors the only ones who are called and who are in ministry? Certainly you've said yes to being a teacher, but in your mind this is just a job in the church that needs to be done. You do like working with children, youth, or adults, or maybe you are a teacher by profession, but you didn't really think of this as a calling or ministry of the church when you agreed to do it.

What do we mean when we say that teaching is a calling and a ministry of the church? Why is it important to see the work of a teacher from this perspective? What do we discover about the importance of this work when we frame it in this way?

Teaching as a Calling

My belief that our work as teachers in the church is a calling begins with a basic and profound theological statement: God calls. The God of the Judeo-Christian tradition is a calling God. We see this in the opening pages of the Old Testament, where God literally speaks and calls the world into being. This act of calling continues in the covenant created with the Israelites as the chosen people. As Sara Covin Juengst reminds us:

> Being called was a part of the covenant relationship. To be an Israelite meant to be subject to that call. The covenant was more than just a contract, an exchange of goods or services; God's people were more than just "hired hands," who would serve God in return for God's protection and favor. God called, and the people responded to that call not out of duty, but out of a sense of unity and belonging. They were called to be God's people.[1]

It is important to remember, too, that the call was to all the people, not just to a few select leaders.

The image of God as one who calls does not end with the Old Testament but can be seen throughout the New Testament as well. Jesus, at his baptism, heard the call and claim of God on his life. As one who manifested the nature of God in his very being, Jesus' own ministry was a calling ministry, one that began with a call to the disciples to come and serve and continued throughout his life on earth and beyond as he called and continues to call those who meet him to new life and hope.

---

[1]Sara Covin Juengst, *Equipping the Saints: Teacher Training in the Church* (Louisville: Westminster John Knox Press, 1998), 20.

The understanding of God as one who calls is also seen as foundational in the early church. It is evident that the early Christian community understood itself as called into being by God through Jesus Christ, called to be Christ's body and presence in the world. Paul reminded the Ephesians of this as he urged them "to lead a life worthy of the calling to which you have been called" (Eph. 4:1). It is worth noting that the Greek word for church, *ekklesia,* literally means a gathering of citizens called out. At the heart of the Christian faith is a belief that God calls us out and asks us to join in God's ongoing creative and redemptive work in the world.

As members of the church, we are part of the body of Christ. We have a place and a task in that body. Our positive response to the invitation to teach is an expression of our willingness to hear and accept God's call and to participate in the larger ministry of the church. Teaching is not just an extra job we've taken on or an additional time commitment we've made. It is a way of expressing our commitment and loyalty to the One who created us, redeemed us, and now calls us. We need to see our service as teachers in the church not as a duty we engage out of guilt or as a burden we must bear but as truly a call from God.

Our use of the word *calling* with regards to teaching in the church also helps us to remember who is really in charge. While the invitation to be a teacher generally comes through others, our faith says that it is God who is asking us to give of ourselves in this vital work of the church. God is the initiator, inviting us to join in God's life and work in the world. This is what a call to teach is all about–saying yes to God's invitation to join in the life of the church, to help pass on the stories of our faith, and to help create openings in people's lives in order that they might come to see and know God who is calling them, too.

Teaching as a Ministry

Donald Griggs boldly claims that teaching is the church's first ministry.[2] While I believe that the church's first ministry is to worship and praise God, it is clear to me that the ministry of teaching is at the heart of worship and praise. How do we know what worship and praise mean and how to do that appropriately unless we are taught? Teaching is indeed a vital ministry of the church.

But you may be struggling with seeing your teaching as a "ministry," or yourself as a "minister." It is ironic that Protestants—especially my denomination, the Christian Church (Disciples of Christ)—place much emphasis on the priesthood of all believers, yet we act as though the only ministers are those who are ordained. In my experience, most laypeople when asked if they are called to some ministry of the church will usually respond with, "Oh, no. I'm not a minister. I'm just a layperson."

I want to challenge that perspective and remind us that our call to ministry comes not through the act of ordination but through our baptism. It is in baptism that we accept God's claim on our lives and take on the name of Christian—Christ's ones. With that commitment comes the responsibility to work and serve in and on behalf of the body of Christ. Saying "yes" to teaching in the church is saying "yes" to being in ministry.

An important question to ask at this point, then, is: What does it mean to call something a ministry? What is "ministry"? Why is it helpful to see teaching as a ministry rather than just as another job in the church?

---

[2] Donald Griggs, *Teaching Today's Teachers to Teach* (Nashville: Abingdon Press, 2003), 13.

We have some clues as to what ministry means when we think about how we use the word. In religious circles, when we talk about *ministry* we generally link it with the word *service.* We talk about someone "serving" in ministry and that ministers are called to "serve." We also use the term in another way and we can see this in the wider social context. In government, especially in countries other than the United States, we often hear the word *ministry* used in reference to a government office and the head of that office is seen as a minister who "represents" the government. For example, a Minister of Agriculture is seen as the representative of government who is responsible for functions related to the agricultural needs of the country. If we put these two perspectives together, we arrive at an understanding that ministry has to do with serving and representing. The work of ministry is to serve and to represent.

When we think of teaching as a *ministry* of the church, we remember that in the midst of our tasks of sharing information, telling stories, and passing on the tradition, we are called to serve and care for those whom we teach. Our students are not objects that we fill with knowledge, but people who need to know they are loved and that they matter to us and to God. We not only talk about God's love and care but we model it in our own actions. We model in many ways, from the hospitality reflected in having our classrooms clean, prepared, and ready when our students arrive, to the caring attention revealed in knowing something about them, their lives and interests, to the concern expressed when someone is absent from a session. One of the saddest things I have heard a Sunday school teacher say is that so and so hasn't been in class for several weeks but she doesn't know why. A simple call to find out how the student is and saying we missed you is an important act of service that any teacher can do.

Understanding our teaching as ministry also helps us remember that we are there on behalf of the church, the body of Christ. We are Christ's representatives when we enter that classroom. As teachers, we are called to be what Kenda Creasy Dean and Ron Foster call "Godbearers,"[3] those who incarnate God's love and who witness to the work of God in their own lives. It isn't about knowing it all or being an expert on the Bible and our faith tradition. It is about bearing witness to the love and grace of God that we have experienced in our own lives. Serving and representing—such is the ministry of teaching!

Summary

My goal in these brief pages has been to help you see your work of teaching as a calling and a ministry that is vital to the church. It still may feel like a challenging and daunting task, and so it should. You have taken on a responsibility of great importance to the body of Christ, and sometimes it can feel like a demanding, frustrating, and thankless job. There are times in the church when we behave like some of the lepers described in Luke 17:11–19. Ten lepers came to Jesus for healing and he healed them all. But only one returned to say thanks. In the church, we, too, forget to say thank you to those who guide and serve and care for us through the ministry of teaching.

Not all of us will burn with passion for the task. It seems like God uses us in spite of ourselves. But, as I pointed out in the Introduction, this is not new. God's call has often been met with resistance and doubt as to whether one has the ability to do it. The amazing thing is that God keeps calling ordinary people like you and me, and ordinary people continue to respond in faith.

---

[3]Kenda Creasy Dean and Ron Foster, *The Godbearing Life: The Art of Soul Tending for Youth Ministry* (Nashville: Upper Room Books, 1998).

If you like to learn, place a high value on teaching and learning, care about people and enjoy being with them, and trust that God in Christ will be with you on the journey, the ministry of teaching can be an exciting, challenging, growing, and fulfilling task. Most importantly of all, God does not expect perfection, that you can be all things to all people, know everything, and know how to do everything. No, all that God asks of us is faithfulness. Out of our faithfulness comes hope for the future of the church.

Further Reflection

1. What led you to say "yes" to teaching? In what ways do you see God at work in this?
2. On a continuum of 1 to 10, with 1 representing "not at all" and 10 representing "totally," rank yourself in terms of how much you feel "called" to teach. Using the same continuum, rank yourself in terms of how clearly you see your teaching as ministry.
3. What difference does it make to think about yourself as called to teach? What difference does it make to think about your teaching as a ministry?
4. How has the church helped you understand and claim teaching as a calling and a ministry? What more might it do?

2

Who Is a Teacher?

"You are a teacher when you share yourself and your faith with others."[1]

It was the first Sunday of the new fall church school program. The hallway was filled with chatter and energy as parents came to collect their children after Sunday school. As one young first grade boy left his classroom, his mother asked him if he liked his teacher. The boy hesitated a moment and then replied, "I didn't have a teacher, I just had a friend."[2] From my perspective, the teacher of this young child has made a good start in modeling for him who a teacher is. Certainly those of us who teach want our students to see us as their friends and through us to see Jesus and God as their friends, too.

However, the question "Who is a teacher?" begs a broader answer than just that teachers are our friends. Having explored what it means to understand our work as a calling and a ministry, I invite you now to reflect on who a teacher is, to look at some of the important qualities that are present in

---

[1]Donald Griggs, *Teaching Today's Teachers to Teach* (Nashville: Abingdon Press, 2003), 42.

[2]Ibid., 37.

effective teachers, and to consider some of the significant roles teachers play in their work. We will begin, however, with a brief look at who and what a teacher is not, at some of the myths about teachers and teaching in the church that cloud our perspective and get in the way of effective teaching. Some of the ways we think about teachers are not always helpful and prevent the church from doing an adequate job in its teaching ministry. Naming these myths helps us dispel them. In all of this, my hope is that through these reflections you will be better equipped to undertake this vital call and ministry to which you have said yes.

Myths about Teachers and Teaching

When we think of a myth, we think of an imaginary story, a fantasy that is not based on fact. When I talk about the myths we have about teachers and teaching, I am talking about those perceptions we have that may not be rooted in fact but have come to hold sway in our thinking. The problem with such myths is that they hinder our ability to see who a teacher is and what teaching is all about. While they may hold a kernel of truth, as myths often do, they keep us from seeing the whole picture. I want to name three such myths that I've seen at work in the church.

The first myth is that *only those who are experts can teach*. This usually shows up in one of the first responses we hear when we ask a person to consider teaching. The response is, "Oh, I can't possibly teach. I don't know enough about the Bible (or the church or being a Christian) to teach." The assumption being expressed is that you have to know it all in order to teach. You have to be an expert!

While I certainly want teachers to know something about the material they are teaching, to assume that only those who have considerable knowledge about the Bible can teach in the church leads us to miss one of the most important aspects about a teacher. First and foremost, a teacher needs to be a learner. Good teachers are those who are passionate about what they are teaching and want to learn more about it. As a church school teacher, you don't need to be an expert, but you do need to care deeply about the Bible and want to learn about it. You need to care deeply about the church and want to learn more about what it means to be a Christian. When faced with the limits of your knowledge, one of the best things you can say as a teacher is, "I don't know. Let's find the answer together." Instead of your expertise, it is your excitement at learning that will be contagious and your students will want to learn more, too.

The second myth is *teachers only work in classrooms.* We seem to think that teachers have to be in classrooms, sitting around tables or standing at a lectern talking. Maria Harris says this limits our understanding of education to only one of its forms, schooling. She comments, "In this view, the participants in education are always 'instructors' or 'learners,' the place of education is necessarily a school; the stuff of education is books and chalkboards and lesson plans; and the process involved is mental activity."[3]

As a teacher in the church, you probably will spend much of your time with your students in a formal structured classroom setting, but it is important to remember that your role as a teacher continues beyond those walls. As Donald Griggs says, "Teaching is more a matter of an opportunity and intention to be in relationship with others and to offer love, insight, and good news."[4] Your relationship with your students outside of the classroom is a part of the teaching process, too.

---

[3]Maria Harris, *Fashion Me a People: Curriculum in the Church* (Louisville: Westminster/John Knox Press, 1989), 39.

[4]Griggs, *Teaching Today's Teachers,* 20.

Sending them birthday cards, sitting with them at a church dinner or during worship, occasionally attending an important school event, calling to inquire about them when they are absent—all of these take place outside of the classroom and are ways we model the good news of God's love and grace for our students. It is important to remember that teaching is not just what teachers do in classrooms. In the final analysis, "Teaching is what the church does by the way it lives and acts."[5] It is what teachers do by the way they live and act.

The final myth is *teachers need lots of students.* Too often I've heard about teachers who become discouraged and finally stop teaching because only one or two students show up on Sunday morning. Or there are small membership churches who have only a few children and youth and conclude that they can't really offer Christian education because they don't have enough people. An underlying assumption seems to be that we need a certain number of students in order to teach.

The culture in which we live contributes to this myth. It is a culture that values size—the bigger, the better. The church is not immune to this cultural value so we also tend to measure worth and success by numbers. The curriculum resources we use in teaching often reinforce this through the assumptions they make about class size. When a teacher is told to divide the class into groups of four and she only has three students, she wonders what she is supposed to do and whether there is something wrong with her class.

Please don't misunderstand me. I celebrate having lots of students in the church, people of all ages who are learning about the Bible and the Christian life. But I want to counter the sense of failure a teacher can have when only two or three students are there on a given Sunday morning. I believe that

---

[5]Ibid., 20.

we can see this as an opportunity, rather than a problem. It is an opportunity to teach in different and creative ways. It is an opportunity to provide lots of individual attention to each student, to have the time and space to be a mentor and friend. It is an opportunity to discover their individual interests and build teaching activities around their interests and needs.

Before we give into the myth that teachers need lots of students, let us remember that we follow the One who never seemed concerned about numbers. Jesus celebrated the shepherd who left the ninety-nine to find the one lost sheep, the woman who searched diligently for the one lost coin, and the father who welcomed with open arms the one lost son. He had one of his most amazing teaching moments with the lone Samaritan woman at the well. Our work as teachers is not about numbers, it is about faithfulness and caring deeply about our students, however many we have, and the good news we have to share.

Qualities of a Teacher

When I ask people to describe a teacher in their lives who had a significant impact on them, they seldom talk about the specific content the teacher taught them or how skilled the teacher was at teaching methods. Instead, I hear a list of the teacher's personal qualities: she was excited about what she was doing; he had a great sense of humor; she was a good listener; he lived what he taught; she seemed to really care about me. Certainly there are skills teachers in the church need to develop and we will talk about these later in this book, but I have come to the conclusion that being a teacher has as much to do with qualities of being, with who you are, as it does with what you do. What are some qualities we find present in those who are effective teachers in the church? I would like to highlight six: (1) a commitment to Jesus Christ,

(2) self-awareness, (3) the ability to listen, (4) an openness to learning, (5) patience, and (6) faithfulness.

For teachers in the church, one of the most vital qualities is a commitment to being a disciple of Jesus Christ. It may seem I'm stating the obvious, but I think it is important to say it. We cannot invite others into a way of life that we have not accepted and are not living ourselves. It is the truth of the old adage: "Actions speak louder than words." To teach in the community of faith, we need to have committed ourselves to learning from Jesus, to growing in our own spiritual life, and to living out our commitment to Christ in our daily walk.

This doesn't mean we have to be perfect. All of us sin and fall short. We all live under the grace of God. However, it does mean that we seek to have our walk match our talk, understanding that our lives are living witnesses to the way of Jesus. It has been said that our students may not study the Bible as diligently as we would like but they do study the lives of the adults around them. Living as a disciple of Jesus Christ is an important quality of a teacher in the church.

A second quality of a good teacher is what I call self-awareness. By "self-aware," I do not mean that you only think about yourself and only look out for "number one," as the narcissism of our culture seems to invite. Instead, I am talking about the ability to be self-reflective, to think about who you are and what you bring as a teacher. Good teachers know who they are and the ways in which this shapes what they do. As Parker Palmer reminds us, "We teach who we are."[6]

In another book, I talk about this as "knowledge of self."[7] As I mentioned in that work, we need to be aware of our gifts. You may think that teaching is all about technique and skill,

---

[6]Parker Palmer, *The Courage to Teach: Exploring the Inner Landscape of a Teacher's Life* (San Francisco: Jossey-Bass, 1998), 2.

[7]John M. Bracke and Karen B. Tye, *Teaching the Bible in the Church* (St. Louis: Chalice Press, 2003), 45–49.

and are concerned that you do not have the necessary skills. I believe that skills are something that we can learn, but it is the particular gifts we each bring to our teaching that help us be effective teachers.

When I talk about gifts, I am referring to the particular qualities of being that we bring to our teaching task. Some teachers are more effective speakers, while others are better at listening as their students voice their opinions. Some teachers seem to naturally know when and how to speak a challenging, prophetic word, while for others it is easier to offer a sympathetic word of care. None of these are better than or more important than the others. Instead, as the apostle Paul reminds us, all of our gifts are given "for the common good"(1 Cor. 12:7). Being aware of our gifts enables us to concentrate on the task at hand, which is using these gifts, the unique qualities of being each of us already possess, for the sake of our teaching and the benefit of our students. Charles Foster says it well: "These gifts are the source of our blessing and the means of God's grace."[8]

A third quality of a good teacher is being a good listener. Too often we think of teaching as a speaking task. A good teacher is therefore one who can talk easily and fill the teaching space with words. In my years of teaching, I have decided that before we fill up our lesson time with our own words, we need to have done some careful listening.

I admit, being a good listener is not easy, especially when you have something important to share. In our culture, what passes as listening is too often what I call "waiting to speak." Just listen to talk radio and take note of how often people talk on top of each other. There is no space between comments for processing what has been heard and truly responding to what

---

[8]Charles R. Foster, *The Ministry of the Volunteer Teacher* (Nashville: Abingdon Press, 1986), 19.

was said. Good teachers, though, know how to pay attention, to truly listen and hear, not just with their ears but with their whole beings.

An important question to ask is, "To whom and to what do we need to be listening?" As we've just discussed, we need to listen to ourselves and have some sense of who we are and what we bring to the task. And we need to listen to our students and be aware of who they are. We need to listen to the questions, concerns, needs, and interests that they bring. It does little good to be busy providing answers to questions that our students haven't even asked! We need to listen to our content, our subject matter. In the church, one of our primary subjects is the Bible, and as teachers we need to spend time in its pages, listening carefully to the witness and testimony it provides. Finally, we need to listen to God, being attentive to God's presence and work in our own lives, in the lives of our students, in the church's life and in the life of the world. Prayer is one of the primary ways in which we listen to God, and it needs to be a vital part of our preparation as teachers.

Another quality of an effective teacher is an openness to learning. A good teacher is at heart a learner. She is excited about exploring her faith, knowing more about the Bible, discovering what the Christian life is all about, and growing in her spiritual journey. A good teacher realizes that, while he is called "teacher" and those with whom he works are called "students," everyone is a learner!

Often when I ask teachers in the church why they teach, they will respond that they teach because they learn so much. They find joy in sharing with others what they've learned. I think it is important to remember, however, that our work as teachers is not to just transfer our knowledge to our students. We call this the "banking" approach to teaching, where we see our task as teachers as simply to "deposit" what we know in others.[9] Instead, I think our work as teachers is to share what we know in a way that invites others to explore it, too. Like the woman at the well (Jn. 4:1–42), we invite others to come and see and to discover the good news of Jesus Christ for themselves. Our openness to learning becomes a gift that enables others to learn, too.

A fifth quality of a good teacher is patience. It is not easy to practice patience as a teacher. In a culture that seems to be driven by the tyranny of the urgent, we are easily caught in the pressure to do it *now*, solve every problem *now,* see results *now,* have it happen *now.* If our students don't immediately catch on to what we are saying or see the point of a biblical story or change behavior we have called into question, we think we have failed. We become frustrated and discouraged and sometimes want to give up.

The thing we need to realize is that change and growth take time. Think of how many times you had to repeat the process of tying your shoes before it became natural. The same thing is true of our Christian walk. We did not learn all that we know about the Bible and living a Christian life overnight and our students won't either. By embracing patience as an important quality of a teacher, we are able to live with the reality that we are in this for the long haul. We are planting seeds for the future of the church and are called to the faithful, patient nurture of those seeds. I often say that I teach for the benefit of my grandchildren and those who will follow them. While I may not immediately see the results for which I hoped, without the patient, regular sharing of what we know and the ongoing modeling of the Christian life, there is little hope for growth.

[9]Paulo Freire, *Pedagogy of the Oppressed,* trans. Myra Bergman Ramos (New York: Continuum International, 2000), 71–86.

While we have certainly not exhausted all the qualities of an effective teacher, the final one I want to mention goes hand in hand with the attribute of patience we just discussed. It is the quality of faithfulness. Much of what makes a good teacher is her or his ability to show up, to be there each Sunday (or whenever you teach), to be on time, prepared, and ready to welcome your students.

They say that 90 percent of life is simply showing up, and the older I get, the more I believe this is true. Effective teachers in the church know that their faithful presence week in and week out is an important teaching in itself. It provides a sense of continuity that many of our children and youth need in order to grow and thrive in a culture that shifts and changes daily with the rise and fall of the latest fad. It models the steadfast faithfulness of the God we worship and serve. It reflects the truth of the psalmist's words, "For the LORD is good; / his steadfast love endures forever, / and his faithfulness to all generations" (Ps. 100:5). While your "yes" to teaching is not a lifetime "sentence" with never a Sunday off, it is a commitment that calls for your faithful response to the regular, often quite ordinary work of helping to guide and form the people of God.

Roles of a Teacher

In addition to naming some of the qualities a teacher needs to possess, it is also important to consider the kinds of roles a teacher is called upon to play. Sometimes I imagine the work of a teacher as a kind of one-person show. It's not that the teacher is always center stage and that the spotlight needs to be on him or her. No, the drama imagery helps me understand that a teacher is asked to assume multiple roles when working with students. Just as an actor in a one-person show must be versatile and take on the characteristics of several personalities, a teacher also performs several vital and necessary roles in encounters with students.

There are many ways we can name these roles. Donald Griggs talks about friend, God's messenger, translator, curriculum writer, and learner as significant roles.[10] In an earlier work, I talk about the roles of partner, companion, midwife, sponsor, and guide.[11] As you think about your call as a teacher in the church, what are some of the roles you are called upon to play as you serve in this important ministry? I want to highlight four significant roles here: an asker of questions, a story linker, a guide, and a partner. While not exhaustive of the roles you will undertake in teaching, these are certainly vital to the task before us.

Asker of Questions

The story about the little boy who asks his mother where he came from regularly raises a chuckle in me. The mother, thinking, "Aha, I've been waiting for this!" launches into the "birds and the bees" speech she has been organizing in her mind in preparation for this moment. After a few minutes of listening to his mother talk about human sexuality and the biology about where babies come from, the little boy gets a puzzled look on his face. The mother pauses and asks her son if he understands what she's been saying. The little boy replies, "Well, Sammy says he comes from Cleveland and I just wanted to know where I came from." This story always reminds me that as teachers we can get caught up in the myth of needing to be the expert, providing answers to questions no one has asked. Even more importantly, we forget that one of the most important roles we play as teachers is that of asking the right

---

[10]Griggs, *Teaching Today's Teachers,* 37–41.
[11]Karen Tye, *Basics of Christian Education* (St. Louis: Chalice Press, 2000), 96–100.

question and helping our students come to an answer that is meaningful to them. If the mother in our story had asked her son, "What do you mean, 'Where do you come from?'?" she would have understood the question he was asking, and thus be able to provide a more meaningful answer for him.

One of the good things about this teaching role is that it calls on you to utilize one of the most important resources in a teacher's toolbox: questions. "Questions are the least expensive resource for teaching and yet may be the most valuable resource available to the teacher."[12] Questions are a primary method of teaching. They are readily available, cost nothing, and can be used with all ages. But they do require some thought and preparation.

There are different kinds of questions[13] that we use in teaching, and knowing which kind to ask and when is an important skill. There are *information* questions. These are simply what the term says—questions that ask for information. Examples include: "What are the books of the Bible?" "In Luke 2, where did Joseph and Mary go to be registered?" and, "What are the "fruits of the Spirit" in Galatians 5:22–23?" This type of question asks for basic information and is important in helping us get a sense of what our students are remembering.

A second kind of question is the *analytical* question. Analytical questions push students to go deeper and invite them to think more critically about what they are learning. Such questions do not assume a right answer and are more open-ended, with the possibility of different responses. They encourage students to go beyond a mere recall of facts and information to an analysis of what those facts and information might mean. Examples

---

[12]Griggs, *Teaching Today's Teachers,* 113.

[13]For further discussion regarding the use of questions in teaching, see Griggs, *Teaching Today's Teachers;* Richard Osmer, *Teaching for Faith* (Louisville: Westminster/John Knox Press, 1992); and Thomas R. Hawkins, *Loving God with All Your Mind* (Nashville: Discipleship Resources, 2004).

include: "Why might Moses have been reluctant to return to Egypt to free the Hebrew people?" "In what ways do you think the church today is like the church Paul was addressing in his letter to the Galatians?" and, "What do you think Mary was feeling as she traveled to Nazareth with Joseph?"

Information questions and analytical questions alone are not enough, so there is another type of question, the *integrative* question. Integrative questions ask students to relate what they are learning to their own lives and to say what it means for them. Like analytical questions, there is no single right answer and the questions are broad and open-ended. They encourage students to go beyond just information and analysis and to seek ways to apply their learnings to their own lives. Examples include: "If you had been one of the shepherds on the hill side in Luke 2, what would you have done?" "In what ways do you see the fruits of the Spirit present in your own life?" and, "Like Moses, to what act of liberation might God be calling you?"

To teach is to ask questions, to give thought and care to the kinds of questions we ask. To teach is to hold before us always the image of Jesus, the one we call the master teacher, the one whose teaching was characterized by the asking of questions. We see this when we look at his encounter with the lawyer as told in Luke 10:25–37. The lawyer comes seeking answers, yet Jesus tells a story and ends it with a *question*: "Which of these three, do you think, was a neighbor...?"(v. 36) The lawyer had to think about his answer. To this day, Christians continue to ponder that question and its meaning for their lives. To be a teacher is to be an asker of questions!

Story Linker

It seldom fails. Whether with my grandchildren or a group of adults in a Sunday school class, the words, "Once upon a time...," or "Let me tell you a story," grab their attention every time. We love stories. At our core, human beings are storytellers. It is through our family stories that we learn something about who we are. Stories are an important way in which we make sense of our world. The stories we hear in church help us understand what it means to be a Christian. The Bible stories we tell over and over again help to connect us to those generations who have gone before us, to remind us who and whose we are. Telling stories is an important part of teaching in the church.

While "storyteller" seems fairly obvious as a significant role for a teacher, the term "story linker"[14] may be new to you. I like the term because it reminds us that our work as teachers involves more than just telling a story. We also help people make links to a story, help them make connections that are meaningful and helpful to them and their lives. Neuroscience is helping us understand how important connections are for the brain and its ability to remember something. It is easier for new information to be retained if the brain sees a connection with something it already knows. Providing links between the biblical stories and our students' stories is important work for the teacher.

Providing a link with a biblical story calls for us to help our students see themselves in the story. The biblical text becomes a kind of mirror through which we see ourselves reflected. Whether a child, a youth, or an adult, the biblical text offers us insight into who we are and why we are here. With children, however, it is important to keep simple the links we help them make. For example, with the story of the wise men's visit to Jesus in Matthew 2:1–12, asking them to think about a time they gave a special gift to someone and

---

[14]I am grateful to Anne Streaty Wimberly for introducing me to the concept of story linking. See Anne Streaty Wimberly, *Soul Stories: African American Christian Education*, rev. ed. (Nashville: Abingdon Press, 2005).

then asking them to think about a gift that they would bring to the young Jesus can help to forge a link with this story that helps children begin to see that being a Christian involves our giving to others.

As a story linker, it is important to remember that your goal is not simply to transmit to your students the links you have made. While it is certainly appropriate to share the connections you see in a biblical text and how that helps *you* understand its meaning, students need to make their own links. That is why the role of asker of questions goes hand in hand with the role of story linker. Asking questions that help students name their own stories and find their own connections is a vital part of story linking. Good questions are an important tool in the hands of a story linker and provide guidance in the forming of connections that will sustain a faithful life.

Guide

There is an old Teutonic word for "teacher" which also means "index finger." It is an interesting image to associate with a teacher. We often use our index finger to point something out to someone or to point the way they need to go. We can use the same words to describe a guide. Simply put, a guide is one who shows the way. Like an index finger, an effective teacher is one who points things out to her students, points the way for them to go. One of our significant teaching roles in the church is that of guiding, pointing the way.

My husband and I enjoy traveling to different countries and exploring different cultures. One of the things that make these travels rich and rewarding experiences is the presence of a good guide. Guides are the ones who help us see significant signposts, who provide commentary on what is happening and why, and who help find answers to questions as they arise. A good guide is also able to navigate detours when they arise and welcomes these spontaneous moments for the rich and meaningful teaching opportunities they can offer.

Like a good tour guide, an effective teacher helps us see what is significant, provides commentary on what is happening, helps us interpret what we are experiencing, and assists us in finding answers to our questions. Like all good guides, an effective teacher has checked out the "trail" ahead of time, has studied the topic and the text under consideration, and knows something of what students will see and experience. He's done his homework!

It is important to emphasize that an effective guide is one who makes the journey with us. She does not stay on the sidelines or sit and wait at the end of the journey. Like Jesus with the two disciples on the road to Emmaus (Lk. 24:13–35), the teacher as guide walks with her students, points out the signposts on the way, witnesses to the gospel in her own life, and celebrates the good news in theirs.

Partner

The final teaching role I want to discuss picks up on the image of "walking with." Partners are those who walk with each other and who work together toward a mutual goal. Partnership is characterized by a sense of mutuality, acceptance, and equal regard. As a partner to his students, a teacher understands himself as one who works with them and walks along side of them, not as one who stands aloof and apart from them. It is as a partner that a teacher is able to see herself more readily as a learner in the midst of other learners. In this role, a teacher is able to see that her students have something to teach her, too.

Partners work together to build each other up in love. Being a partner with our students as we seek to walk in the way of Jesus helps us to see that our students are not objects that we must manipulate and shape into a particular mold and fill up with all the right answers. Teaching as partnership reminds us that we share the power of learning with our students and work with them in order that we might all, like Jesus, grow in wisdom and stature and favor with God (see Lk. 2:52).

In his wonderful collection of children's stories, *Does God Have a Big Toe?* Marc Gellman tells the story of "Partners." It is, in his words, a "midrashim," a story about a story in the Bible. In this instance, it is a story about Genesis 1 and the creation of the world. In Gellman's telling of the story, God invites the man and the woman to be partners in the finishing of the world. When the man and woman ask, "What's a partner?" God answers in this way: "A partner is someone you work with on a big thing that neither of you can do alone. If you have a partner, it means that you can never give up, because your partner is depending on you."[15] It is a big thing we are working on with our students, helping them become disciples of Jesus Christ. We depend on each other in order to stay faithful to that task. Being a partner with our students in the mutual work of learning what it means to be a Christian is a foundational role for our ministry as teachers!

Called to be an asker of questions, a story linker, a guide, and a partner—these are some of the vital roles a teacher plays. While each of us who teach will "play" these roles differently and bring our own unique personalities to the task, they are important and necessary roles in the ministry of teaching and call for our committed and faithful efforts.

Summary

So, who is a teacher? An effective teacher possesses several qualities and is able to embrace a variety of roles. Her

---

[15]Marc Gellman, *Does God Have a Big Toe?* (New York: HarperCollins, 1989), 3.

effectiveness begins with the ability to live beyond some of the myths that cloud our vision of teaching in the church. She realizes that she does not need to be an expert in order to teach in the church. She does need to be passionate about learning. An effective teacher understands that his teaching occurs not just in the classroom but extends beyond those four walls into other opportunities to encounter and interact with his students. He knows he teaches as much by example as by what he says. Finally, an effective teacher does not get caught up with numbers and the need to have lots of students. She rejoices as much with two or three students as she does with a roomful, and knows that where two or three are gathered together, the Spirit will be present and at work (see Mt. 18:20).

While each teacher is unique and brings her own particular skills and gifts to her teaching, effective teachers reflect some common qualities. An effective teacher in the church is a disciple of Jesus Christ, seeking to grow and mature in his own Christian walk. An effective teacher is self-aware and knows something about what her unique gifts for teaching are. An effective teacher is a good listener and realizes that teaching is not all about the teacher talking. An effective teacher is open to learning, recognizing that his own passion to learn can be contagious. An effective teacher is patient, allowing the time and space for change to happen. Finally, an effective teacher is faithful. One of the most significant tasks of a teacher is regularly showing up, on time, prepared, and ready for her students. Our students come to understand the steadfast faithfulness of God because of a teacher who is steadfast and faithful in her work.

Teaching also calls us to play a variety of roles. We are askers of questions, knowing that answers are dependent on the questions that are asked. We are story linkers, helping our students learn the stories of faith, make connections between these stories and their personal stories, and find meaning and guidance in these connections for their daily lives as Christians. We are guides. Like an index finger, we help to point the way, offering direction and assistance on the Christian journey. Finally, we are partners who join with our students in the activity of learning, recognizing the mutuality of the teacher/student relationship and understanding that we have things to teach each other.

Who is a teacher? In the community of faith, a teacher is an ordinary human being who responds in faith to the extraordinary call of God to share herself, her faith, and her passion for learning more with others. We are shaped by certain qualities and called to carry out certain roles. All of this we do with humility and grace, recognizing that it is not all up to us, and trusting always in the faithful presence of the One who calls and who will guide our steps.

Further Reflection

1. Think about a teacher who shaped your life. How would you describe the teacher? What qualities made him or her a good teacher? Which of these qualities do you see in yourself?

2. Compare the list of qualities of this teacher with the list offered in this chapter. What similarities and differences do you see? What additional qualities would you add to the list?

3. What qualities do you bring as a teacher? What unique gifts do you have to offer? Make a list of these, give thanks to God for them, and celebrate them!

4. Review the various roles of a teacher. Which of these feel most comfortable to you? Which one challenges you?

5. Are there other roles you see yourself playing as a teacher? Name these and think about why they are important to teaching. Add them to the list.

PART TWO

Teaching Practices

"Teaching is less about doing 'great things' and more about 'doing small things with great love.'" [1]

We've come to an important point in our exploration of your calling as a teacher. Thus far we've talked about teaching in the church as a calling and a ministry. We've reflected on some of the important qualities of a teacher and thought about the various roles a teacher plays. Another way to think about this is that we have looked at the *what* of teaching (it's a calling and a ministry) and the *who* of teaching (who a teacher is). But we cannot be faithful in this important ministry for our church unless we also ask the question, *How* do we teach? What are the key elements that go into the actual act of teaching?

I like to think of the things we do as "teaching practices." Most of us are familiar with the word *practice*. We've all heard the classic folk wisdom, "Practice makes perfect." Many of us can still hear our parents' voices reminding us to practice our piano lesson (or whatever instrument we played). These uses of the word all point to doing something repeatedly so

---

[1] Sam M. Intrator, *Stories of the Courage to Teach* (San Francisco: Jossey-Bass, 2002), 34.

we become good at it. I certainly want us to practice our teaching so we become good at it! But the concept of practices (the plural form) invites us to think about practice in another way. This use of the word reminds us that there are customary actions and behaviors that make up the work of teaching, there are "practices" that effective teachers do. Just like a doctor "practices" medicine, a teacher "practices" teaching.

In part two of this book, we explore some of the key practices of effective teachers. We look at methods and tools a teacher uses in these practices with the hope that you, the reader, will become adept at them in your teaching. In the following chapters, we explore four practices I consider to be critical to the work of a teacher. These are (1) the practice of knowing our students, (2) the practice of knowing our subject matter, (3) the practice of creating a learning environment, and (4) the practice of planning and preparing lessons.

Knowing Our Students

I praise you, for I am fearfully and wonderfully made.
    Wonderful are your works;
that I know very well. (Psalm 139:14)

"Remember: we teach people, not lessons." This is a statement I make regularly to my seminary students as we think about the ministry of teaching in the church. Knowing our students is one of our most important teaching practices. Paying attention to the people we teach is basic to our work. To teach effectively we need to know something about our students: who they are, where they come from, what matters to them, how they learn, and so on. We won't discover all of this overnight, but knowing that we need to pay attention to who our students are helps us grow in our understanding of them as we continue to teach.

We automatically pay attention to some things when we meet someone. We ask them: What is your name? Where are you from? Where do you live? With children and youth, we will ask where they go to school and what they like to do. With adults we often ask where they work. Besides these questions, we also take note of physical characteristics. Are they male or female, tall or short, child or adult, or do they belong to a particular racial or ethnic group? The list goes on.

The difficulty comes when we begin to form a judgment about our students based on the superficial things we see and hear. The assumptions we make take hold of us and we stop seeing our students for who they really are. They become simply a category to whom we relate. A normal toddler becomes a "terrible two"; a very active and energetic nine-year-old becomes a "hyperactive child"; and a thirteen-year-old becomes "a hormonal teenager." When we jump to judgment too quickly, we miss the rich complexity of individuals and often miss opportunities to help them grow in their Christian faith in ways particular to them.

My purpose in asking us to think about who our students are and to recognize this as a vital teaching practice is to get us to look beyond the surface. My invitation is to think carefully about our students, who they are, and how we can be effective teachers and guides for them.

We could fill a whole book about what we need to know about the students we teach. So, where do we start? For me there are some basic things that are particularly important and helpful to effective teaching. First, we need to look at the complex nature of being human. Second, we need to consider the process of human development. And third, we need to think about how people learn.

The Complex Nature of Being Human

I chuckle every time I recall the story about the two neighbors who were talking one day about how much they loved the children in the neighborhood. Later in that day, one of the neighbors heard the other yelling at some of the kids on the street. Going to investigate, he discovered that his neighbor was upset because one of the children had tossed a ball into some freshly laid concrete in his driveway. When the neighbor with the damaged driveway was reminded by his friend that they had been talking about loving the children, he responded: "Well, yes, I love kids, but in the abstract and not in the concrete!"

It is a funny play on words, but it reminds us that it is easier to think about people in the abstract, in terms of generalities, and relate to them as categories: senior adults, high school youth, infants and toddlers, and so on. We even use such categories to group people in our church schools. While these groupings can be helpful, we need to be mindful that people do not come in the abstract but in the particular. Our students come in all sizes and shapes. They are complex and multidimensional in nature, and "one size" does not fit all.

However, some common aspects of this complex nature of being human influence how we teach. Even though each student will reflect these common aspects in different ways, these commonalities still provide a lens through which we can see our students and deepen what we know about them. I want to explore three: the biological, the psychological, and the cultural aspects of being human.

It is important to remember that our students are biological beings. They come in a particular gender (and there *are* differences between males and females); they have certain physical abilities and limitations; they are a certain number of years old; and they are changing and maturing as they grow. Because of our biological development, we are able to do different tasks at different times in our lives. For example, small children do not have highly developed fine motor skills. This is especially true of young boys. Asking them as a part of a Bible lesson to do a craft exercise that requires lots of small movements and manipulations with their fingers will often be an exercise in frustration for them. However, engaging young children in whole body movements, like acting out a Bible story, will be much more compatible with their biological development.

Let's not forget that adults are biological beings, too. As teachers of adults, we need to be sensitive to their needs. Research shows that both sight and hearing decline with age and to ignore this can hinder our older adults from enjoying the fullness of learning. As teachers, we need to check to see if they can hear us and whether they can see the blackboard if we are using one. It can be helpful to enlarge the print on any handouts we use in class.

Biological factors affect the learning process at any age. Recent research reports on adolescents suggest that they are not getting enough sleep. But this may be due to more than just staying up too late or trying to cram too much into a day. Brain research is suggesting that teenager brains may actually function on an internal time clock different than adults.[1] When most adults are waking up and getting ready to go to work, teenagers are just getting down to serious sleep. The lack of youth energy for a Sunday morning Bible study class may have as much to do with biology as it does with interest and motivation. Changing the time when we schedule Bible study with them may be an important teaching move. Paying attention to the biology of those we teach is a vital part of the practice of knowing our students.

It is also important to remember that our students are psychological beings. Psychology looks at the emotional and behavioral characteristics of a person. To talk about students as psychological beings highlights that they each have a different personality and relate to the world and each other in different

---

[1]See, for example, Gaia Vince, "Teenagers: Lost in Time," Newscientist. com News Service, September 2, 2006. Available at: http://www.newscientist.com/channel/being-human/mg19125672.000-teenagers-lost-in-time.html.

ways. This isn't a unique or new insight, and I'm sure many of you are nodding your heads, yes, and saying, "Of course." It may not be a new insight, but, as effective teachers, we need to pay attention to it.

Let's illustrate how this plays itself out in a teaching context. In any given classroom, we will have those who are very talkative and outgoing, often have their hands up to answer the question before you've even finished asking it, always want to go first, have very high energy levels, and can dominate class conversations. Then there are quiet students, those who don't speak unless spoken to, who hold back when you begin a new activity, who want to sit and watch rather than actively participate. Finally, other students fall somewhere in between these two ends of a spectrum. To complicate matters, you as a teacher fall somewhere in this mix, too.

We must remember that there is nothing wrong with any of these students, or with yourself. We are just different and relate to and respond to our world differently. It is the responsibility of a teacher, however, to find ways to include each of these students. For the quiet students, we need to provide opportunity for them to enter the class discussions. One of the ways I do this is to ask students to make sure at least three other people have spoken before they speak again. Even children can do this kind of self-monitoring. This tends to slow down the more talkative and provide some room for the quieter ones. Another technique is to use small groups for some discussions. The quieter students often find room to contribute in these smaller settings. For shy students, it is also less intimidating to talk to three or four people rather than a full classroom.

For the outgoing and energetic students, it is important to have active experiences, to provide variety, and to help them channel their energy in useful ways. Sitting still for long periods of time will not benefit them. There also needs to be ample time for discussion for some of our more talkative students. Sometimes they are doing their thinking out loud and need time and space to do this. We may need to help them listen to themselves because they are so busy talking they don't hear what they are saying. Reflecting back to such a student what you just heard them say is a helpful teaching strategy.

Not only do we as teachers need to recognize that people have different personalities and respond in different ways, we also want to help our students see this and appreciate the differences. Inviting students to see each other as bringing unique gifts to the community of learning will help them recognize how much they can learn from one another. It is taking seriously the apostle Paul's call to the church to recognize that it is the body of Christ and every one is welcome and needed.

Finally, it is important to recognize that our students are cultural beings. We all have a cultural, or social, heritage as well as a biological one. We begin learning this heritage from the moment we are born so that our cultural perspectives seem as natural as our breathing. Who we are as persons is influenced and shaped by our families and communities, the environments within which we grow and develop, the manners and traditions we learn, the television we watch and the music we hear, the values we are taught. We learn particular ways of behaving, of interacting, even of seeing the world. And we bring our particular cultural perspective to the learning moment.

If we are to be effective as teachers, we need to pay attention to the cultural dynamics at work, both with our students and with the content we are teaching. Let me give you an example. One of my seminary students was serving as a teacher of junior high age youth in a local congregation. He prepared a Bible study on the story of the golden calf, told in

Exodus 32. He wanted his young students to think about idols and look at the idols in their own lives. From his perspective and from the perspective of the text, idols were a negative thing and created barriers between people and God. As we explored his lesson plan, I asked him the question: What would be the first thing those junior high youth would think of when they heard the word "idol"? He thought a moment and replied, "*American Idol,*" the popular TV show. We understood that to these youth an idol was not a negative thing but something toward which our culture aspires. If my student hoped to effectively teach these junior high youth, he needed to at least understand how they might initially hear the story in order that he might help them understand the biblical text and draw some appropriate meaning from it for themselves.

Cultural awareness is vital to effective teaching. It plays an important role when we are teaching the Bible. We need to be aware not only of our particular cultural perspective and how that shapes what we hear in the scripture we are reading. We also need to know something about the cultures that formed those very same scriptures. People who lived in very different places and times than ours wrote the Bible. To enter its pages is like entering a foreign land. If we as teachers are not aware of this and have not helped our students be aware of this, then understanding what the Bible may be saying to us today will be more difficult.

For example, our Western culture places a great deal of emphasis on the individual. It is about individual rights and what is best for each person. This cultural perspective means that it is easy for us to read the pronoun "you" in a biblical text and hear that as speaking to me, an individual. We think of "you" in the singular form of the pronoun, meaning one person. Often in the text, however, the reference is to "you" plural, meaning "you all." The declaration in Matthew 5:14, "You are the light of the world," is not just about individuals but about communities–congregations–being light to the world. What we miss because of our cultural perspective is the biblical concern for community, for "we." As teachers in the church, we are called to recognize the role culture plays both in our students' lives and in the scriptures we teach.

The teaching practice of knowing our students calls us to be aware of the complex nature of what it means to be human. We recognize the particular, unique nature of each person in our community of faith. We take note of the various factors–such as biology, psychology, and culture–that shape and influence each person in his or her growth and learning. In so doing we are better able to make a place for all people as we teach and learn.

Understanding Human Development

Human beings develop. A child is not a miniature adult. We grow and change throughout our lives. In order to effectively teach, it is helpful to know something about human development, especially about how our students are developing cognitively–meaning, in their ability to know something.

Our students are cognitive beings, which says that they are capable of knowing and constructing knowledge. But they do this in different ways at different ages in life. Jean Piaget, a Swiss psychologist, was fascinated with how people know. As he watched his own children grow and develop, he became aware that they processed things differently at different ages. Out of his observations he developed a theory of cognitive development[2] that helps us understand what is happening with our students as they learn.

---

[2]To read in greater detail about Piaget's theory, see Jean Piaget and Barbel Inhelder, *The Psychology of the Child* (New York: Basic Books, 1969), and Hans Furth, *Piaget for Teachers* (Englewood Cliffs, N.J.: Prentice-Hall, 1970).

Piaget observed that our mental abilities evolve and expand across time from birth into adolescent years and beyond. Infants and toddlers in what Piaget calls the sensorimotor period are limited in their ability to engage the world. They grow to recognize themselves as an object distinct from other objects in their environment and they develop an awareness of their immediate space and some sense of time. But they struggle with what we call representational thought, e.g., knowing that the word *cat* represents a certain animal. Their use of verbal language is limited. For teachers of children at this age, trying to "teach" or instruct them about Bible stories is not a particularly helpful activity. The most important thing a teacher can do for very young children is to let them know they are loved and that this community of people can be trusted. We can certainly share simple Bible verses about God's love and faithfulness with them, trusting that they will become aware that this book we read is important even if they don't understand it.

A child in what Piaget calls the preoperational stage of development (approximately two to seven years of age) begins to use representational thought. Language skills develop and she or he starts to speak in fairly complex sentences. But children this age have difficulty differentiating among truth, fantasy, and realism. It is easy for them to believe that an elephant like the Disney cartoon character, Dumbo, can fly. Their concept of space and time is still limited and categories like past, present, and future are difficult to understand. To talk about Jesus living two thousand years ago holds little real meaning for children in this age. Trying to teach them a complex biblical concept like grace or salvation is not particularly helpful. One of the best ways to teach the Bible to preoperational children is to share biblical stories with them, but avoid trying to make a point or saying, "The meaning of this story is…" We don't need to be so concerned about the children getting it "right." If we build a foundation of love and respect for the Bible, the children will develop meanings as they are ready.

The stories we share at this age need to be chosen carefully. There are many that can be quite frightening to children, like the sacrifice of Isaac told in Genesis 22. When teaching the Bible to children, we need to ask, "What will the children hear in this? How will they interpret it?" Young children hear a statement such as, "I have Jesus in my heart," and wonder, "How did he get inside of me? Did I swallow him?" An effective teacher thinks about how preoperational children will hear the story before she teaches it.

The next stage in Piaget's theory is the concrete operational stage. From ages seven to eleven, children begin to evolve into logical thinkers and are able to carry out cause and effect thinking. They can perform what Piaget calls "mental operations," including reasoning, being aware of variables in a situation, and understanding the relationship between parts and whole. Concrete operational children can hear the Bible stories as a part of the bigger story of God and God's people. They have a sense of history that was lacking in the previous stages. But they can also still be literalists. They think concretely and it is easy for them to read the Bible as a factual history book, becoming frustrated when the facts don't agree.

In the formal operations stage (ages eleven to fourteen and beyond), the young adolescent is developing the ability to do conceptual thinking. He or she can imagine a range of possibilities, create theories, think of time and explain infinity, and think symbolically. If we have done our work well as teachers in the earlier stages of cognitive development, we will discover young people at this age able to engage in serious and thoughtful study of the Bible that helps them draw meaning for their own lives from the text.

To know our students means we are aware of their developmental journeys. We've focused on cognitive development here because of the critical role it plays in our students' readiness to learn and in how we teach. However, the important thing to remember in all of this is that our students are changing, growing, dynamic people and our work as teachers calls us to relate to them where they are in their journeys.

How People Learn

It is a moment we all anticipate as teachers. We can see it in our students' faces or in their eyes. It is a like a light bulb has been turned on and they can see. It is that "Aha!" experience when you know they get it. It is the moment of learning. When it happens, all the hard work of teaching suddenly becomes worthwhile.

We want our students to learn. We want to teach in ways that help them to learn. In order to do this, it is important that we understand something about the human brain and how it works. It is also helpful to think about learning styles, what they are, and how they shape the way we learn.

The Human Brain

If we are going to think about how people learn, then we have to think about the brain, our primary organ of learning. While much is still unknown, research has uncovered a lot of knowledge about the brain in the past few years, some of it very helpful to teachers. With neither time nor space to go into great detail, let's look at some "brain basics" that can be useful for those of us who teach in the church.

We begin our journey into the brain with an illustration[3] to help us glimpse its major systems. Imagine your extended index finger pointed toward the ceiling. Place this finger through the hole of a donut. Over the extended finger and the donut place a tissue that covers them. Here you have a simple model of the human brain. The index finger presents the oldest part of the brain, the brainstem and the cerebellum. Our brainstem controls many of the body's automatic functions, such as the circulation of blood and breathing. The cerebellum maintains the body's balance and muscle coordination.

The donut represents the limbic system, which is wrapped around the brainstem. This part of the brain is fully realized only in mammals. There are some very important structures located here, including the hippocampus, the amygdala, the thalamus, and the hypothalamus. These structures communicate chemically with every cell in the body. This part of the brain plays an important role in learning, which we will talk about in a few moments.

The tissue represents the newest part of the brain, the cerebrum and neocortex. As you can see from the model you've created, this part of the brain sits atop the other two systems and is what distinguishes humans from other animals. In the actual brain, it is the largest part and houses an amazing amount of specialization. Thought, speech, our ability to plan and make choices all reside here.

Hopefully this brief tour of the brain gives you some small sense of the richness and complexity of this organ. It is said that our brain is far more complicated and sophisticated than any currently conceivable computer. It does so much more than receive data and do some simple processing of it. This

---

[3]I am grateful to Thomas R. Hawkins, *Loving God with All Your Mind,* (Nashville: Discipleship Resources, 2004) for providing me with the idea for this illustration.

is why the banking approach to teaching, where we only seek to fill our students heads with data and facts, is not especially brain-friendly.

But there is more to know biologically about the brain that is useful for those of us who teach. It is 78 percent water; eight gallons of blood flow through it every hour; while it represents only 2 percent of our body's weight, it uses 20 percent of the body's energy; and it is the only organ in the body that can't store energy.[4]

Why are these facts helpful to a teacher? Knowing that the brain is 78 percent water reminds us how important hydration is to the brain. I like to think of water as one of the important brain foods. Keeping our students regularly supplied with water helps keep their brains in good working order. When we think about the blood flowing through the brain, we recall that oxygen is transported via that flowing blood. Oxygen is another absolutely vital brain "food." One of the ways we help move blood through our bodies is through physical activity. To provide opportunity for our students to be physically active and moving during our teaching experiences helps supply their brains with fresh oxygen, keeping them alert and aware.

Finally, the brain needs energy, lots of it, yet it cannot store fat. It must rely on a regular supply of food energy from outside itself. Nutritionists often tell us that breakfast is one of the most important meals we eat. One of the reasons for this is the need to replenish the brain's energy after the body has gone several hours without food. It makes a difference in students' ability to concentrate and learn as to whether they have been able to eat breakfast before they arrive for Sunday school. It matters, brain-wise, as to whether they have had proper nourishment on a regular basis.

---

[4]The brain has no way to store fat, which provides energy for the body. This is probably a good thing because the addition of fat in the brain would literally lead to a "big" head, and there is no room for such growth inside our skulls!

What else do we need to know about the brain in order to be more effective teachers? Another helpful fact is that the brain is composed of 100 billion neurons, or nerve cells. I have heard that there are more neurons in each of our brains than there are trees on the planet earth. These neurons are key to our learning. Through chemical transmitters, our neurons connect with or "talk to" other neurons to form what are called neuronal networks. It is these networks that are the structures for learning.

Our neuronal networks are formed by repeated behaviors and experiences. For example, a child sees a dog for the first time. His father points to the dog and says "dog." At that moment the child's brain makes an initial connection. Some of the neurons in his head are processing this interaction and relating the object, a dog, with the sound his father makes. The next time the child sees a dog and hears his father say "dog," his brain will use the same connections. After continued encounters with dogs and hearing the word, the child's brain will easily make the association. If the dog barks, the brain makes an additional connection that this object called a dog makes this particular sound. After continued encounters with barking dogs, the child's brain will quickly make the association. We can say the child has learned that this is a dog and it barks. Each new thing the child experiences with dogs–wagging tail, licking tongue, and so on–is added to the neuronal network associated with dogs. The more the network is used (that is, the child encounters dogs), the stronger the connections will be and the easier it is for the child to recall what a dog is.

This same process is at work with our students in church. The first time a child hears a Bible story, some initial connections are formed in the brain. Repeated encounters with the same story will strengthen those connections and make it possible for us to say the child has learned the story. It becomes a part of the neuronal networks and is easy for the child to remember. This is why visiting the same stories again and again is helpful in our teaching the Bible to children.

Even with all those billions of neurons, our brains still face far more stimuli than they can process. The question then becomes, how do our brains decide what they will focus on? What helps the brain of that child, youth, or adult listening to a Bible story decide it will pay attention to it?

Existing connections are one of the key criteria the brain uses to determine what it remembers. The hippocampus, located in the limbic system of the brain, plays a key role here. It functions much like a file manager. When we encounter new data, it first looks to see if we already have a "file," a neuronal network associated with that data. It is easier for the brain to attach new data to already existing information than it is to create a new neuronal network. It takes a lot of repetition to create a new network.

For teachers, there are some important things to note about the role that connections play in how the brain learns. First, we need to think about the connections we are putting in place when we are teaching. Let me illustrate. I once heard a children's sermon based on Matthew 10:26–39. It is a complicated text that first deals with fear and Jesus' assurance that we have nothing to fear. God even knows the number of hairs on our heads! The second part of this text deals with the cost of discipleship and talks about Jesus having come to set man against father and daughter against mother, and says that whoever loves son or daughter more than Jesus is not worthy of him. My fear as I sat there listening was what connections the children would make with this text. Would they remember the assurance that in God we have nothing to fear or would they hear that Jesus comes to separate them from their parents, certainly a fearful thought to a child? I was somewhat relieved when a parent of one of the children reported to me later that her daughter had been fascinated with the idea that God knew the number of hairs on her head. It was a good connection but it could as easily gone the other way, with the children hearing and believing that Jesus comes between them and their parents.

When you teach, think about the possible connections your students might make. Your work as a teacher is to help them make appropriate and meaningful connections. For teachers of young children, I encourage you to think twice about using a text that can cause problematic connections. A young child does not need to know all the Bible all at once. You will have time to work with the more difficult texts as children and youth grow and develop.

The second thing we need to know is what connections are already in place. Our students do not come to us as blank slates. Their brains already have neuronal networks in place. Their hippocampus works to connect what they are learning with what they already know and sometimes those connections can be difficult. Recall my earlier story about the young teacher who wanted to talk about idols with his junior high students. They already had a neuronal network in relation to idols and would approach any new learning initially through that network. If the teacher is to help them make appropriate connections and draw useful meaning from the stories about idols in the Old Testament, he needs to have some sense of the students' existing connections. The teaching principle here that guides my own work is that *we begin with what our students know and not with what we know.* As teachers, we need to think about what our students already know as we prepare to teach.

Besides connections, the brain uses another important criteria in deciding what will capture its attention. The amygdala, also found in the limbic system, plays a key role here. It is busy scanning all of the new data for its emotional content. It is asking the key question, Does this matter to me? Does this hold any emotional significance in my life? If it doesn't, or if a teacher cannot help the student see why it might be important and matter, the brain will be less attentive to the material.

The key here is that it has to matter to the student. Even though it may matter to you as the teacher, what counts it is the emotional significance it holds for the student. Going back to the teacher with the lesson on idols, he needs to help his students see why talking about idols as a negative factor in their lives might matter to them, especially in the midst of a culture that celebrates being the *American Idol*. Otherwise, they will probably tune out.

There is another aspect of the brain's use of emotion in its learning process that is critical to our work as teachers. It is what I call the challenge/threat line. The brain needs challenge. Challenge and stimulation are important brain "nutrients." Boredom is deadly and leads the brain to stop paying attention. As we teach, we need to be challenging our students' brains through providing a variety of experiences, introducing novel and new ways of looking at things, offering a wide range of sensory stimulation, and providing as enriched a teaching environment as possible.

However, we cannot ignore a caution here. If, in providing challenge, we cross over into threat where our students feel unsafe, then we have created a problem. Threat diminishes the brain's capacity to think and learn. When feeling threatened, the brain tends to revert to that part of the brain that has been called the reptilian brain, the brainstem and the cerebellum. One of the primary purposes of this part of the brain is to keep us alive. Generally this is done through three options: we fight, we flee, or we freeze. Just think of a wild animal. When confronted with danger, the animal will either turn and fight, will run away, or will freeze in place, hoping the danger will go away. In important ways, we humans do the same thing. This is a problem when we are teaching.

Let me illustrate. Some years ago, I first heard a musical rendition of Psalm 23 recorded by Bobby McFerrin.[5] I thought the music and words were beautiful. Composing in honor of his mother, McFerrin used feminine images for God, talking about God as "She." I decided to use this piece for a Bible study I was teaching. I thought everyone would love it as much as I did. To my surprise, the song raised a great deal of resistance. Some in the class immediately began to argue that God was not a woman (the "fight" response). Some simply withdrew (the "flee" response). I could see in their faces that they were no longer engaged. Others looked like deer in headlights (the "freeze" response). They didn't know what to do. In introducing new language for an old and treasured scripture, without any attempt to prepare them ahead of time, I had crossed these students' challenge/threat line. Until they felt safe again, learning would be difficult. We had to spend a lot of time in that Bible study talking about the experience and letting them express their responses freely and without judgment before we began to move to a place of openness to learning again. Awareness of the challenge/threat line in our students' brains is vital for effective teaching.

All of these insights about the human brain have led me to formulate and use some basic principles when I teach:

- Begin with where the students are.
- Teach to and for connections.
- Remember the important role that emotion plays.
- Teach to challenge and not to threaten.

[5]Bobby McFerrin, "The 23rd Psalm," *Medicine Music,* EMI-USA CDP7-92048-2.

While these do not automatically guarantee effective teaching, they do represent a brain-friendly approach to our work and are significant in our knowing who our students are.

Learning Styles

In his delightful children's book, *A Walk in the Rain with a Brain,* Edward Hallowell reminds us, "No brain is the same, no brain is the best. Each brain finds its own special way."[6] I think we are all aware that each of us has our own special way of learning, our own unique pattern by which we perceive and process the world around us. We call this a learning style. Learning to teach to a variety of learning styles is important to being an effective teacher.

One of the big factors in a learning style is how we like to receive data and information. Some of us are more *visual* and like to see what it is we are learning. We want to read the biblical text, not just hear it. We want maps of the places we are studying. We need visual resources such as pictures, charts, graphs, and actual demonstrations we can watch. Others of us rely more on our ears and hearing. We call these *aural* learners. We like to listen to lectures and want to hear the biblical text read aloud. We more easily remember something we've heard than something we've read in a book.

Then some of us who are known as *kinesthetic* learners. We are people who need to move around, use our whole body in the learning process. We need to be doing something, touching something, handling something in order to be fully engaged. Even if we have to sit still and listen, some part of our body needs to be moving, like swinging our feet.

---

[6]Edward Hallowell, *A Walk in the Rain with a Brain* (New York: HarperCollins, 2004), 24.

I've often wondered whether some of the children who are labeled hyperactive are simply kinesthetic learners who find themselves restricted in environments that want them to be quiet and still. There are also *interactive* learners, those of us who need the interaction with others in order to really pay attention. We need the opportunity to verbalize out loud what we are thinking and to talk it through with other people. We find small group discussions or talking to the person next to us to be very helpful. To be constantly told to be quiet is a frustrating experience for these learners.

Not only do we take in the information we are learning in different ways, we also seem to have different ways in which we process it. Let me illustrate. Some of us seem to work best when we can think about something in a logical, sequential manner. We like our information presented in an orderly and organized way. Others of us seem to like brainstorming and working in a more spontaneous manner. We don't mind if things don't fit together in an orderly fashion. Some of us want to sit back, observe, and reflect about the information before we respond in a discussion. We are doing our thinking first inside our heads. But others need to immediately begin talking and will be the first out of their chairs to take part in an exercise. They seem to be thinking out loud as they go along.

All of the approaches I've described represent different ways in which we learn. Generally we use elements of several of these approaches in our own learning style. In addition, we find ourselves to be what Hallowell in *A Walk in the Rain with a Brain* calls "smart" in different ways. Some of us seem to have a gift with words. Others are quick to see a pattern, how something relates to something else. Still others show a talent for anything musical. Then there are those who seem particularly sensitive to the feelings of others. These are among the capacities that Howard Gardner identifies as "intelligences."[7]

The important thing to remember here is that no two students approach learning in exactly the same way. And we, as teachers, have our own approach to learning; we tend to teach to our own learning style. Since we learn this way, we assume others learn that way, too. To be effective teachers, however, we need to work at expanding our own approach to learning in order that we can engage more fully the variety of ways our students learn. By doing this we honor the different ways people learn and make room at the educational table for everyone.

Summary

Knowing our students is an important teaching practice. Understanding something of the complex nature of what it means to be human, recognizing that our students are at different points in their developmental journey, and having some knowledge of how they learn all play a vital role in effective teaching. We know our students are biological, psychological, and cultural beings. We know that their capacity to know and understand changes as they grow and develop through the years. And we realize that people learn in different ways. As those called to teach in the church, we celebrate our students and commit ourselves to the practice of knowing as much as we can about them. Then we, too, like the psalmist, can declare that we are fearfully and wonderfully made and give thanks for such a gift (Ps. 8:3–9)!

---

[7]Howard Gardner, *Frames of Mind: The Theory of Multiple Intelligences* (New York: Basic Books, 1983). For a useful summary of Gardner's work, see Jerry Larsen, *Religious Education and the Brain* (New York: Paulist Press, 2000), 124–30.

Further Reflection

1. Think about the three dimensions of human beings: biological, psychological, and cultural. As a teacher, which of these are you most aware of as you teach? Which dimension do you need to give more thought to?

2. What did you learn about the brain from reading this chapter? What do these learnings help you see about yourself and your students?

3. Review the list of guidelines for teaching with the brain in mind. Which ones do you use now? What additional guidelines would you name? Add them to the list.

4. Describe your own learning style (visual, aural, kinesthetic, interactive, or a combination). How does your style influence the way you teach? How can you become familiar with all the styles in order to use them in your teaching?

4

Knowing Our Subject Matter

Therefore my people go into exile for want of knowledge…
(Isa. 5:13a, RSV)

A radio show on National Public Radio that I listen to on occasion on Saturday mornings is Michael Feldman's "Whad'Ya Know?" It's a funny show, filled with lots of interesting trivia and information. The program is designed to exercise our memory and see how much we are in touch with some of the more interesting but not always headline stories in the news. It always begins the same way. Feldman asks the studio audience the question, "What do you know?" They respond, "Not much. You?" I generally chuckle when I hear that response because I know that in the program that follows, both the studio audience and listeners will reveal how much they really do know.

Maybe one of your hesitations when asked to be a teacher in the church was a concern that you don't know enough. You may think, "Not much," as you reflect on what you know about the Bible, and wonder if you should have said yes to teaching. This same hesitation may be present as you begin to read this chapter. If one of the key practices of teaching is to know your subject matter, you think, "I'm not qualified and should have said no."

Let me provide a word of hope by reframing this practice slightly. I believe this teaching practice is about *learning* to know our subject matter and not about already being an expert. It is helpful to me to remember the words of Parker Palmer: "The subjects we teach are as large and complex as life, so our knowledge of them is always flawed and partial."[1] While we certainly need to know something about the subject we teach, Palmer reminds us of the humility needed when exercising this practice. It is impossible to know everything and teachers are not expected to. One of the exciting things for me about being a teacher is how much I continue to learn! Our knowledge of the subject matter is always a work in progress. The key to this teaching practice is a commitment to our own ongoing learning.

So what does this practice include? One of the ways we could answer this question is to explore the things we think Christians need to know in order to be faithful disciples of Jesus Christ. Our list would probably include the Bible and its stories, Jesus and his ministry, who God is and how God works in our lives, the church and its mission, our own denominational heritage, what it means to live as a Christian today, the disciplines of the Christian life, an awareness of other religions and cultures, and the list could go on. But to explore all of these so we "know our subject matter" would take volumes and we only have a few pages!

Let me focus on two key aspects of this teaching practice of knowing our subject matter that are significant to me and may be helpful to you. First of all, when we talk about knowing our

---

[1]Parker Palmer, *The Courage to Teach: Exploring the Inner Landscape of a Teacher's Life* (San Francisco: Jossey-Bass, 1998), 2.

subject matter, what kinds of knowing are we talking about? And second, as Christians we are called "the people of the Book." We claim that the Bible is central and authoritative in our life. It is our core subject matter. Therefore, what do we need to know about the Bible?

Kinds of Knowing

As teachers, I think it is obvious that we want our students to learn, to come to know something. I think we would find some agreement about what it is we want our students to know. We want them to know about the Bible, its stories, its history, and its teachings. We want them to know about God and Jesus. We want them to know about the Christian life.

The key word here is *about.* When our emphasis is on knowing *about,* we are focusing on what I call "propositional" knowledge. This kind of knowledge emphasizes facts and information, assuming that if we know *about* something or know *that* something is thus and so, we therefore know it. When we spend a lot of time helping children learn and memorize Bible verses, we are engaged in propositional knowing. We assume that they know John 3:16 if they are able to recite it correctly; or that they know the story of the good Samaritan if they are able to tell it correctly with all the details in order.

There is certainly nothing wrong with propositional knowledge. We do need to know about the Bible and what it says. We need to know about God and Jesus and the church if we want to call ourselves Christians. I think having children memorize some Bible verses is quite useful and provides them with a basic knowledge of the text that is important as they grow in their faith.

The issue is that knowing *about* something isn't enough. Knowing about Jesus and his life and ministry is certainly important, but we need to know more. We need to know *how* to live as Jesus would have us live. We need to be able to witness in our own lives to Jesus' ministry and mission, not just with words but with actions. We need our students to know what it means to serve "the least of these" (Mt. 25) in our world today.

I call this kind of knowledge "active" knowledge. It reminds us that we need to ask not only what our students need to know but how they need to know it. It reminds us that teaching is more than just learning about something, and that good teaching also helps us learn the skills and behaviors required to live as Christians in the world. "Knowing how" is knowledge that comes from lived experience and the practice of new behaviors and new attitudes. "Knowing how" means as teachers we not only teach out of books but we teach with hands-on experience that helps our students learn how.

My seventh-grade church school teacher was a woman who seemed to instinctively understand about knowing how. The class was a group of young adolescent girls, most of whom had been raised in the church. Many of us had memorized numerous Bible passages in our summers spent in vacation Bible school. We knew a lot about the Bible and knew about its teaching that Christians were called to serve others. We had a lot of propositional knowledge. But Mrs. K. knew that we needed more than this. We needed to know something about how to serve others. To do this, she had the class "adopt" an elderly woman in the church as our class grandmother. We called her "Grandma P" and she was confined to her home, was blind, hard of hearing, and showing signs of diminished mental capacity. As a group we went to see her on several occasions, made small gifts for her, and regularly prayed for her. Suddenly, serving others was not an abstract idea we learned about during our hour in class on Sunday morning.

Instead, serving was the hard yet rewarding work of relating to and caring for Grandma P as we coped with her various limitations. The content of our Sunday school lessons became an important "knowing how."

Thomas Groome says it well: "The fool or ignorant one in the Bible is not the person who does not 'know about' intellectually, but rather the one who fails to do God's will."[2] It is not enough to know about the Christian life. We need to be able to live it as we respond in faithfulness to the will of God in our lives.

Another kind of knowledge plays an important role in our teaching. In addition to propositional knowledge and active knowledge, teachers in the church need to be sensitive to what I call "appropriate" knowledge. Particularly with children, we need to be sensitive to the appropriateness of a given biblical text for the students we teach. As I said in the previous chapter on knowing our students, we need to ask how our students might hear a particular story, what connections they might make, and what are the various ways they might interpret it. An important question to regularly ask is, Is this an appropriate text to be teaching these students at this time?

While I certainly believe that the Bible as a whole holds wisdom and insight for us and that it is important to wrestle with its difficult passages and stories, I also believe there are appropriate times in our growth and development when we are better able to do that kind of wrestling. For a young child, stories such as the command to sacrifice Isaac (Gen. 22), or the assassination of Sisera (Judg. 4), or Jesus' teaching that whoever loves son or daughter more than him is not worthy of him (Mt. 10:37) can be frightening. They are best left for

---

[2]Thomas Groome, *Christian Religious Education* (San Francisco: Harper and Row, 1980), 142.

a time in the children's growth and development when they are able to hear and understand these texts.

The teaching practice of knowing our subject matter involves understanding the different kinds of knowledge. Propositional knowledge, active knowledge, and appropriate knowledge are all a part of what we want our students to learn. Understanding this is an important part of effective teaching.

Knowing the Bible

One of the most exciting aspects of being a teacher is the opportunity to learn more about your subject. For those of us who teach in the church this opportunity includes learning more about the Bible. Coming to know our sacred text is an ongoing teaching practice.

What does knowing the Bible involve? It certainly involves knowing *about* the Bible. We need to know some elementary facts and information about this book that holds authority in the Christian community. Such information would include things like the following: the Bible comprises sixty-six books that are divided into the Old and the New Testament; it was written over a period of more than one thousand years, which means many perspectives, historical moments, and cultural influences are represented in its pages; its content has immense variety, including poetry and prose, long narratives and short stories, legal codes, hymns and prayers, proverbs and wisdom sayings, letters, parables, reports of mysterious happenings, and so on; it was written in cultures very different than our own, so entering its pages is like entering a foreign land; and it is not so much a history book as we understand history as it is a witness to the ways people experienced God and their understanding of who God is and what God is about in the world.

This basic information merely scratches the surface of all there is to learn and know about the Bible. I would like to have time in this book to probe deeper. Since we don't, I encourage you to do so on your own. I have included at the end of this chapter a list of resources that you can use as you work to expand your own knowledge about the Bible. It is also my hope that your church provides ongoing opportunities through adult Bible studies for you to expand your own knowledge about the Bible.

Beside knowing *about* the Bible, I believe teachers need to know *how* to study the Bible. Whether you are using prepared curriculum resources or designing your own lessons, having some good study skills is vital as you work with the biblical text. In seminary circles, we call these *exegetical* skills. The word *exegesis* means to lead out and make known. As a teacher, your goal is to help lead out and make known the texts your students are studying.

Bible study involves more than just reading the passage through a couple or three times as you prepare your lesson. Let me suggest some steps that can help to deepen your understanding and therefore your ability to help make the text known both for yourself and for your students.

1. *Use a good study Bible.* I have listed ones I would recommend at the end of this chapter. A study Bible provides brief background information on each of the books of the Bible, including discussion about authorship, setting, history, audience, and themes. It has notes on each page that offer helpful information about the text you are reading. Most good study Bibles are designed for use by both lay and clergy readers so you don't need an advanced degree in the Bible to be able to use one.

2. *Read the passage through several times.* I find it helpful to read it both silently and out loud. Sometimes I hear things

when I read it aloud that I do not when I read silently. If you have more than one version of the Bible, read the passage in another version than the one you usually use. Take note of differences in translation and think about how a different word affects your understanding of the text. Because translation is a very difficult task, scholars of good faith can disagree on how to translate a word. Instead of worrying about which word is the right one, I find that the differences can help me see something I might not have noticed otherwise.

3. Like a good reporter, *ask questions of the text*. The following are some of the ones I find helpful:

- What catches my attention in the text? What more do I want to know about it?
- What is happening in the text? Who are the main characters? What are they doing? Why?
- What seems to be the subject, theme, or main idea of this text?
- Who wrote it?
- When was it written?
- Who is the audience?
- What is the historical context? What was happening in the wider historical and cultural context at the time?
- What precedes this text and what follows it? How do these seem to relate to this text? (It is important not to isolate a text from the material around it.)

Notice that I begin with questions regarding my own responses to the text. I think this is a good place to begin. But we don't stop there. We see what others have to say, too. That is why a good study Bible and other resources like a Bible commentary, Bible dictionary, and Bible atlas are helpful.

The important thing here is to spend time with the text first, pondering the questions we have, and allowing the text to speak to us. We call the Bible a "living Word" because we believe there is always new insight awaiting in its pages. Thoughtful Bible study involves both our own reflections and the insights of scholars.

4. Finally, *connect what you have learned with your students.* This is the time to think about what you discovered in the text. What insights and meanings do you take from the text? What do you think your students will hear in the text? What kinds of connections will they make with it? (Remember what we learned about the brain!) What does this mean for their lives today?

This is the point also to begin pondering how you might teach this text. We will explore designing and planning lessons in a later chapter, but you can begin to think about this in the midst of your Bible study. Think about: How does what you discovered fit with the curriculum resources you are using? Are there things you would add or do differently? If you are designing your own lessons, what main theme will you pick as a focus? What kinds of teaching methods will you use? How will these help your students learn from this text?

Engaging in these steps helps to deepen your knowledge about the Bible and provides you with greater insight to share with your students. The concern I hear raised by teachers in the church has to do with time. Most of you are doing this on a volunteer basis and live busy lives that involve work, family, and community commitments. Finding time to study the Bible and to increase your knowledge of content is difficult. I understand that. But I also believe our call to teach is an important call and worth our best efforts. Taking some regular time each week to use the steps I've named and to study the text you will teach represents our best effort.

I want to briefly mention one final study skill. It has to do with *hermeneutics.* Hermeneutics is the work of interpretation.

All of us are interpreters of the biblical text. In other words, we read from a particular perspective that shapes what we see and understand. The Bible is read in some common ways, and being aware of these can help us in our work as teachers.[3]

We can read the Bible as though it reflects or describes the world. This way of interpreting assumes that the text is to be taken literally, that it presents a factual account of what happened. For example, we can read Genesis 1 as a text that is literally true and presents a factual, accurate description of how the world began. Some in our churches read the Bible this way, but others no longer understand the Bible as literally and factually reflecting the world.

We can read the biblical text from the viewpoint of the author, seeking to understand who the author was, what circumstances he or she was addressing, and who the audience was. In this approach we would read Genesis 1 and begin to ask questions about when the story was written and by whom, who was the audience and what kind of world did they live in, and so on. This way of reading is referred to as an historical-critical approach and focuses on the historical background—who wrote it, what was going on, and to whom and for whom was it written. The assumption is that understanding something of the text's background helps us understand its meaning.

Another way we can read the Bible is from a literary perspective, focusing on the text itself. This approach to the text looks at the literary features of the passage, its structure, its artistry, and the ways in which it makes its point. Just

---

[3]For a fuller discussion of what follows, see chapter 4, "Issues of Inter-pretation," in John M. Bracke and Karen B. Tye, *Teaching the Bible in the Church* (St. Louis: Chalice Press, 2003).

like reading a good novel or poem, we are drawn into the world of the text and seek to understand it on its own merits. Reading from this perspective, we would take note in Genesis 1 of the repetitions such as, "And God said…," "God saw that it was good…," "And there was evening and there was morning…,"and wonder how these repetitions are important to what the text is saying.

Finally, we can read the Bible from the perspective of the contemporary reader and what we bring with us to the text. For example, when reading the creation stories in Genesis 1 and 2, as a woman I take note of the creation of man and woman and think about how these texts have been used to justify the oppression and domination of women. This approach to reading reminds us that we each bring our own connections, experiences, values, and concerns to the text, shaping what we see and hear in it. We all read the Bible out of our own experience and this colors what we see and what we don't see.

None of these ways of reading, or interpreting, the Bible is necessarily right or wrong. Most of us use some combination of them when we read and study. The important task as a teacher is to be aware of your own reading perspectives and to be sensitive to the interpretive perspectives of your students. Each of these different interpretive approaches asks different questions of the text and helps us see something the other perspectives do not. Only by reading the text through a variety of perspectives are we likely to see the rich insights the Bible is offering us.

Developing good study skills and expanding our awareness of the perspectives from which we read the biblical text are all vital to knowing the Bible. To be effective teachers in the church, we need to know our Scripture and be able to share it in meaningful ways with those we teach.

Summary

As teachers in the church, we are called to the practice of knowing our subject matter. This does not mean that we have to be experts or biblical scholars in order to teach. It does mean that we are committed to continue learning and growing along with our students. It means that we are sensitive to the need for our students to develop different kinds of knowledge. They need propositional knowledge–knowing facts and information about what they are learning. They need active knowledge–knowing how to live the truths they are discovering. And they need appropriate knowledge–knowledge that they can understand and is appropriate for their age, developmental capacities, and where they are in their life journeys.

The practice of knowing our subject matter calls for us to develop good Bible study skills and to spend time each week exploring the texts we are teaching. It means that we develop a sensitivity to the various ways we can read a text and use these ways of reading to enhance our own and our students' learning.

All of this requires time and energy on our part. But it is time and energy well spent as we help our students discover the insights and life-giving wisdom to be found in the Bible, the holy book at the center of our life as Christians. Effective teachers take seriously the practice of knowing our subject matter, recognizing the truth in the words from the gospel of John: "...and you will know the truth, and the truth will make you free" (Jn. 8:32).

Further Reflection

1. In your own teaching, which of the kinds of knowing (propositional, active, appropriate) tends to be your focus?

What can you do to include all of these kinds of knowing in your lessons?

2. What steps do you currently follow when you study the Bible in preparation for your lesson? What will you add or do differently after reading this chapter?

3. What resources and tools do you use in your study of the Bible? What new resources do you see on the list provided that you would like to make use of? Encourage your church to make these resources available in the church library.

Resources for Bible Study

Study Bibles

The Access Bible, New Revised Standard Version with Apocrypha. New York: Oxford University Press, 1999.

HarperCollins Study Bible: New Revised Standard Version. San Francisco: HarperSanFrancisco, 1994.

The New Interpreter's Study Bible: New Revised Standard Version with the Apocrypha. Nashville: Abingdon Press, 2003.

The New Oxford Annotated Bible, New Revised Standard Version. New York: Oxford University Press, 2001.

Zondervan New International Version Study Bible. Grand Rapids, Mich.: Zondervan, 2004.

Zondervan Today's New International Version Study Bible. Grand Rapids: Mich.: Zondervan, 2006.

Other Study Aids

The Concise Concordance to the New Revised Standard Version, edited by John R. Kohlenberger III. New York: Oxford University Press, 1993.

Global Bible Commentary. Nashville: Abingdon Press, 2004.

HarperCollins Bible Commentary, rev. ed. by James L. May. San Francisco: HarperSanFrancisco, 2000.

HarperCollins Bible Dictionary, rev. ed. by Paul J. Achtemeier. San Francisco: HarperSanFrancisco, 1996.

Oxford Bible Atlas, 3rd ed., edited by Herbert G. May. New York: Oxford University Press, 1985.

Introductions to the Bible

Anderson, Bernhard W. *The Unfolding Drama of the Bible.* Minneapolis: Fortress Press, 2006.

Griggs, Donald. *The Bible from Scratch: The New Testament for Beginners.* Louisville: Westminster John Knox Press, 2003.

____.*The Bible from Scratch: The Old Testament for Beginners.* Louisville: Westminster John Knox Press, 2002.

Handy, Lowell K. *The Educated Person's Thumbnail Introduction to the Bible.* St. Louis: Chalice Press, 1997.

5

Creating a Learning Environment

> *"To teach is to create a space in which the community of truth is practiced."*[1]

We walked down the hallway. As we approached the doorway of a classroom, I asked the group of church school teachers with whom I was working to be aware of their impressions—what they felt, sensed, and thought—as we stepped into the Junior High classroom, one of several on our tour through the church's educational facilities. We paused for a moment inside the door and stood in silence as we took in the room painted in a dull green with a long rectangular table in the center surrounded by metal folding chairs. Little broke the monotony of the room, with the exception of a few old posters taped to the wall and a cluttered bookcase in the corner. After a few moments, I invited responses. A quiet voice rose from the back of the group, a gentleman who had taught this class

---

[1]Parker Palmer, *The Courage to Teach: Exploring the Inner Landscape of a Teacher's Life* (San Francisco: Jossey-Bass, 1998), 90.

for some years. He said, "I want to turn and run back down the hall to the nursery. It is filled with color and light, with soft surfaces and bright pictures on the walls, with comfortable places to sit and fun things to do. It is so much more inviting! If I were a kid, I wouldn't want to spend much time in this room. Maybe that's why we find the junior highs hanging out around the nursery door on Sunday morning!" In that moment, the teachers saw the importance of creating a welcoming and inviting learning environment for their students.

As Parker Palmer says, to teach is to create a space.[2] One of the most important teaching practices is the creating of a learning environment. This practice reminds us that context matters. It matters because it is part of what we are teaching. It is part of what educators call the "implicit" curriculum, the curriculum that a school "teaches because of the kind of place it is."[3] For example, we can talk all we want about love and grace and hospitality in the church. If the places where we teach such lessons are not environments of love, grace, and hospitality, it will be difficult for our students to hear what we are saying. It's the old adage about actions speaking louder than words. Space, the environment within which we teach, speaks loudly, too. Such space is a teacher's responsibility. Charles Foster says it well: "It is the teacher who creates the environment of hospitality and grace."[4]

Kinds of Space

To create a good learning environment calls for awareness at two important levels. First, we need to be aware of the physical

[2]Ibid.

[3]Elliott W. Eisner, *The Educational Imagination,* 2d ed. (New York: Macmillan, 1985), 96.

[4]Charles R. Foster, *The Ministry of the Volunteer Teacher* (Nashville: Abingdon Press, 1986), 36.

space, and, second, we need to be aware of the emotional space.

Physical Space

Peeling paint, broken furniture, crumbling plaster, musty smells, old materials crammed onto disordered shelves, general dirt and grime all send a message. They communicate a lack of awareness of the impact that space has on the student and say, "We have not prepared for your coming." We certainly wouldn't welcome guests into our homes without some preparation of the physical space!

We provide welcome space in a variety of ways. Our teaching space should have adequate light, comfortable temperature, furniture, and acoustics that fit the needs of our students. Putting aging adult bodies onto metal folding chairs for any length of time is not conducive to learning. Crowding small children around a table in a tiny classroom with little room for them to move and be able to engage a Bible story through role play and other activities is not conducive to their learning.

We need to remember our discussion about the brain and how it learns. We talked about the need for an enriched environment to stimulate the brain. Space rich with sights, sounds, smells, textures, and tastes helps us learn. We need to attend to all of these in our learning environments.

Preparing an appropriate physical environment does not need to cost a lot of money. I have found that the "coffee table" books they sell at used book fairs are full of wonderful art. These pictures can be cut out, mounted on construction paper, laminated, and hung in the classroom. Organizing a volunteer work group to clean classrooms that have become cluttered can be a good service project for a church with limited custodial help. Inviting artists in the congregation to paint murals on the walls of the children's rooms offers these artists an opportunity to use their gifts on behalf of the church. Asking a carpenter in the congregation to build a loft for reading in the youth room or to construct bookshelves in the children's area is another opportunity for the congregation's gifts to be used. Think creatively and you will be amazed at what can be done with limited resources to develop good physical space for learning.

Emotional Space

Most of us have had the experience of walking into space where we have felt at home and we wanted to sit down and stay a while. We have also had the experience of walking into space where we did not feel "safe," even though there was no evidence of any physical threat. Both of these experiences suggest that space is more than just a physical reality. Space is also an emotional reality.

When we feel unwelcome, afraid to express who we are and what we believe, or threatened by those who seem to hold power, we have a difficult time learning. In such an emotional environment, we are too busy trying to protect ourselves and cannot be as open to growing and learning. Just remember our discussion in a previous chapter about the role of threat and the way it limits the brain's capacity to learn.

The sad thing for me is that such space is sometimes found within our churches. I have been in congregations where I did not feel welcomed, not because people said I wasn't wanted but because they did nothing to include me. I have had people say to me that they are afraid to speak up in a church school class for fear that their beliefs will be ridiculed or put down by both the teacher and other students. The teachers may deny this, but the ridicule does not have to be obvious. It can be as subtle as a roll of the eyes or a deep sigh when someone begins to speak, as though to say, "There she goes again."

What makes good emotional space for learning? I think of at least three qualities of such space. It is hospitable, it is open, and there is a sense of safety. Hospitality is the act of receiving another in an attitude of warmth and care. It is the act of welcoming another. We want people to feel at home and cared about in our teaching spaces. It is important to remember that it is not just the people themselves but also the different ideas and perspectives they bring with them. Hospitality involves both people and ideas. In order to learn and grow, we need to encounter different ways of thinking and be challenged to look at something from a new perspective. In effective teaching environments, the welcome mat is out to both people and ideas, saying, "Please come in, sit awhile, and let us learn from one another."

Openness is another quality of an effective learning environment. When I use the term "openness," I'm talking about an attitude of freedom and mutuality. People feel free to share what they are thinking and feeling, to ask questions, and to wrestle with hard issues without fearing attack or ridicule. To create open space, we need to remove some of the things that hinder learning, like the fear of appearing ignorant. I think it is difficult for people, especially adults, to say they don't know or they don't understand. Yet admitting what we don't know is the beginning of learning, because then we have the opportunity to find out. Teachers who encourage questions, who listen to different viewpoints, who become excited about exploring and discovering with their students, who know that their students may have something to teach them, who are able to say, "I don't know, let's find out together"–such teachers are embodying the quality of openness in their work.

Another quality of an effective learning environment is a sense of safety. We've talked several times already about the role fear plays in the brain's ability to function. Because it is so central to how the brain works, we have to pay attention to safety. People need to feel safe if you want them to learn.

We hear a lot about "safe space" in our world today and struggle, as a society, with the presence of violence in our lives on a daily basis. I think we would all agree that we want to keep physical violence of any kind out of our churches. What we often overlook, though, are the other kinds of violence that can creep in without our notice. When we belittle people, make fun of them or allow others to make them the target of jokes, when we respond with sarcasm, ridicule, and put downs or do nothing to prevent others from doing this, we are perpetuating violence upon others. The old adage, "Sticks and stones may break my bones, but words can never hurt me," is simply not true. Words can be among the most powerful weapons we unleash on another. And the damage done can last a lifetime. Allowing children and youth to call each other "stupid" or to use other terms of ridicule is an example of such violence. As effective teachers in the church, we need to practice creating safe environments, free of violence of any kind and shaped instead by grace, love, and care.

Creating a Caring Learning Community

Attention to the physical and emotional qualities of the space within which we teach is an important part of the teaching practice of creating a learning environment. All of this comes together for me in the work of creating a caring community within which learning can occur and through which we make visible for our students God's care and concern for them.[5] Such work involves four important steps, core elements

---

[5]I am grateful for the work of Charles Foster and his emphasis on the concept of care as central to the ministry of teaching. See ibid., especially Part III, 33–58.

in the practice of creating a learning environment. These steps include: (1) preparing for those who come; (2) greeting people as they arrive; (3) helping people feel at home; and (4) remembering the learning environment extends beyond the walls of the classroom.

Prepare for Those Who Come

When we invite people to our homes for a meal, we prepare for their arrival. Many of us have a checklist in our minds that we use to think about our preparations. Mine includes making sure the house is clean and picked up, getting out the linens and dishes and setting the table, planning dishes I think they will enjoy, shopping for food, and preparing the food. Just before they arrive, I check to see that there is quiet music in the background and the candles are lit.

I believe as teachers we need to have similar checklists in mind as we prepare for our students. Some of these will be things we do every week, and some will be things that need our occasional attention. But all are a part of making sure our students know that we expect them. Following is a checklist[6] that I find helpful as a teacher in preparing for my students:

CHECKLIST FOR PREPARING FOR STUDENTS

- The room is clean.
- The furniture has been arranged in a manner appropriate for today's teaching.
- The temperature is comfortable and the lighting is bright enough for people to see.
- The curriculum materials are out and ready for use when needed.

---

[6]I have adapted a checklist first developed by Foster in ibid., 37.

- The supplies for activities are available for easy distribution.
- The visual aids are placed where they can easily be seen by students and are at their "eye height."
- There are appropriate signs of hospitality, e.g., a pot of coffee, juice and snacks, fresh flowers, etc.
- There are activities for the early arrivals to participate in.
- I have reviewed the lesson plan and am prepared for the day's session.
- There are appropriate signs and people throughout the church to help guide students to the classroom.
- I pray for my students, myself, and for God's guidance in our learning together.
- Other–*add your own items to the list.*

Hopefully the items on this checklist will become second nature for us as we carry out our ministry of teaching. The time we spend preparing for students is an important investment in the overall learning experience and goes a long way toward communicating the gospel of love and welcome we seek to proclaim.

Greet People as They Arrive

Once we have prepared for our students, it is vital that we be there to welcome them. One of the most important commitments a teacher makes is to be there and be ready when the first student arrives. I know that may take a little extra planning on a Sunday morning when you are trying to get a family ready and off to church. But being there to greet our students is a responsibility we undertake when we say yes to teaching. Our welcome reflects the welcome extended by the one we seek to follow, by Jesus who welcomed everyone into the household of God.

The way we greet our students is important, too. If you teach young children, I encourage you to get down on their level to say "hello" to them. It is intimidating to a child to have all these adults towering above them. Being greeted at eye level goes a long way in helping them feel this is a place they belong.

Call your students by name. As the theme song from the TV comedy *Cheers* says, "you want to go where everybody knows your name."[7] Of all the institutions in our culture, church needs to be a place where we are known and called by name. The God we worship and serve has called us by name and claims us as God's own (Isa. 43:1a). As people created in God's image, we, too, are asked to call each other by name and claim each other as brothers and sisters in Christ. Know your students by name and greet them that way!

Help People Feel at Home

We've prepared for our students and we've greeted them as they arrived. These steps in the practice of creating a learning environment lead to our next step, helping them feel at home. Hopefully the signs of preparation and the greeting have already begun to help them feel at home. However, there is still more we can do as teachers.

First, we can display signs of their belonging. This may mean a chart in a prominent place that lists all of the names of the class members. As class members create various works of art in relation to a lesson, we can post these on the walls for all to see. We can invite children, youth, and adults to bring in pictures, posters, plants, and other items that help to make the room their space.

---

[7]Gary Portnoy and Judy Hart Angelo, "Where Everybody Knows Your Name," *Keeper*, Arguntum label, 2003.

Second, we make room for their voices. Too often the primary voice heard in a classroom is the teacher's. Discussions and learning activities in which the students are invited and encouraged to speak their own thoughts and ideas are significant ways in which to let their voices be heard. Teachers do not always need to speak the only or the last word on a topic. There is much wisdom in our students, and making room for them to voice their perspectives is a vital part of helping students feel at home and know they belong.

Third, we help students feel at home by choosing activities that connect with their interests and abilities. With children and youth especially, it is important that teachers know something about their culture, their music, their heroes, and their interests. It doesn't take a mind reader to figure this out. Just ask them! They will be more than happy to be your teacher and introduce you to what matters to them. If you listen with a nonjudgmental ear and express an authentic interest, you can learn a lot about their interests and abilities.

Being sensitive to physical abilities is an important part of helping students feel at home. I have seen craft activities for young children that do not take into account the fine motor skills, or lack of them, especially in young boys. Working with scissors, trying to paste small pieces onto a sheet of paper, stringing beads, and so on are difficult tasks for young ones who have not yet developed the fine motor skills to do these things. It is hard for them to feel at home when they are continually asked to do something beyond their capacity. We do this to adults, too. Many of our senior adults have difficulty reading small print and we can go a long way toward helping them feel at home by providing large print books and handouts that make it easier for them to see. It says we have thought about you and want you to feel a part of this.

Fourth, we help our students feel at home by demonstrating that we care about who they are and what they do. We do this when we celebrate the special moments in their lives. Birthdays, anniversaries, retirements, graduations, earning a driver's license, losing your first tooth, starting first grade—all of these are significant events in students' lives. Taking time in class to acknowledge these says to the students that they matter to us. We also need to be passionate about other accomplishments in our students' lives—acknowledging these, too. When a child reads a Bible passage aloud for the first time in class, we need to notice that and say, "Well done." When a youth risks talking and sharing a significant insight in a class discussion, we need to offer thanks for the contribution. All of these are ways in which we say to our students, "We care about you and you matter to us."

Finally, one of the important ways we can help our students feel at home and create a good learning environment is by establishing a class covenant. I like the biblical image of covenant more than I do a class contract or a list of class rules. Covenant carries with it a sense of mutual responsibility and promise. We all agree together to live and relate in certain ways and hold each other accountable for that. It is the "agree together" that is important. As the teacher, it is not wise to impose a class covenant on your students. Instead, you need to work together to decide what rules of behavior and relationship will guide the class.

Even though we aren't always conscious of them, families have covenants that guide their behavior. As a member of the family, you know what is acceptable behavior and what isn't. Healthy families usually talk about such covenants and are clear about what is expected and what is not. You know you are part of the family because you know the guidelines and live by them.

The same is true of a group or class in the church. The clearer we can be about the rules that will guide our behavior together (things like being on time, treating each other with respect, keeping confidences, not talking when others are speaking, taking turns, etc.), the greater the likelihood that our students will feel at home because they know how to act in this place. Class covenants can go a long way toward helping with discipline problems, too. As a teacher, you have an agreed upon set of guidelines to use to help a student monitor his or her behavior.

Remember the Learning Environment Extends beyond the Walls of the Classroom

The final step with regard to the practice of creating a caring learning community is the need to remember that the context for learning extends beyond the walls of the classroom. As teachers in the church, we will often encounter our students in other places in the church besides the classroom. Just because we are no longer in that setting does not mean that our students will stop noticing us and learning from us. We will continue to be models of discipleship for them.

They will notice whether we pay attention to them, whether we greet them by name, whether we ask what is happening in their lives. They will notice whether we take time to talk with them and treat them with respect. They will notice whether we act as though they are important members of the congregation or not. They will notice if we miss them when they are absent and whether we try to stay in touch through cards and phone calls. They will notice whether we live what we teach.

It is too easy for children and youth to become forgotten and overlooked outside of the context of their particular activities. What we need to remember is that they are as much a part of the church of today as they are the church of tomorrow. As teachers, we are called to continue to welcome and include our students wherever we encounter them.

The teaching practice of creating a caring learning community is a vital and important one. It takes some thought and effort on our part, but it is worth it. Research has long shown that we learn much more than what we hear in words. The environment within which we learn is a part of the content we are learning, too. We need to pay attention to it.

Summary

One of the important practices of teachers is the creation of learning space for our students. To do this we need to be aware of the kinds of space we are creating. We need to attend to both physical space and emotional space. Within this space, we need to take some important steps in order to create a place of welcome, love, and care for our students. We need to take the time to prepare for their coming. We need to be there to greet and welcome them as they arrive. We need to help them feel at home and know that they belong. And we need to remember that the space in which we teach extends beyond the walls of the classroom. Our students are watching and taking note of who we are and what we do wherever they see us. Our teaching and their learning does not end at the classroom door.

The practice of teaching and creating a learning environment takes some time and effort on our part. I know we all lead busy lives, but the effort we give is well worth it. We have the opportunity to incarnate in the spaces where we teach the love and grace of the God we worship and serve. We can live the truth that all are welcomed at God's table.

Further Reflection

1. Describe the physical space within which you teach. What would be a student's first impression when entering this space? What is the emotional climate of this space? In

what ways is it open and safe for the students? In what ways is it not? What needs attention in both the physical and emotional aspects to help it be a welcome space for them?

2. Review the "Checklist for Preparing for Students." Which of these do you already do? Which do you need to work on? What additional things do you need to add to your list?

3. In what ways do you interact with your students outside of the classroom setting? What did this chapter help you remember about these interactions that is important to you?

6

Planning and Preparing Lessons

"Discovery, like surprise, favors the well-prepared mind."[1]

Recall again my reminder to my seminary students: "We teach people, not lessons." I generally add this clarification: "Lessons are simply resources for us to use." We need to keep this focus in mind as we think together in this chapter about planning and preparing lessons, one of the foundational practices of teaching. Our teaching is always about people, which means that sometimes we have to alter and change our lesson. Too often I have heard church schoolteachers express disappointment, even guilt because they weren't able to make it through the lesson on a particular Sunday. Their feelings prevented them from seeing some of the exciting discoveries and learnings that did take place.

But a carefully prepared lesson, as Jerome Bruner reminds us in the quote that introduces this chapter, helps these discoveries,

---

[1]Jerome Bruner, *On Knowing: Essays for the Left Hand* (Cambridge, Mass.: The Belknap Press of Harvard University Press: 1979), 82.

surprises, and learnings happen even when we are not able to finish all we had planned. While we teach people, lessons are still an important tool in our work as teachers and we need to give our best effort to our planning and preparation.

What is a lesson? Charles Foster calls a lesson, "a plan of action for our teaching."[2] I like to think of it as a road map that tells us where we will begin, identifies things to see and do along the way, and provides us a destination toward which we are heading. Teachers in the church tend to use two primary types of lessons. The first is what I call a "prepared" lesson plan that has been developed by the writers of the curriculum resource your church is using. There is generally a teacher's book that outlines the lesson, and the teacher's primary task is to become familiar with it and to make selections among the various activities suggested for use in teaching. The second type of lesson used in the church is what I call the "teacher-created" lesson, where every step of the plan originates with the teacher. He or she decides the theme, the goal, and the activities and resources to be used.

I think many teachers probably use aspects of each of these types of lessons in their teaching. We may begin with a prepared lesson but make adaptations based on our situation and our students. We focus the theme a little differently, we decide that a different insight or goal is more appropriate for our particular students, and we include some activities or resources not mentioned. Or we select a biblical text or issue that we want to explore and then look for various prepared resources that can help us teach it. The outline for the lesson is primarily our own, but we draw on prepared materials as needed to help us accomplish our goal.

Whichever type of lesson we choose to use, some general guides to lesson planning are helpful in carrying out this

---

[2]Charles R. Foster, *The Ministry of the Volunteer Teacher* (Nashville: Abingdon Press, 1986), 82.

vital teaching practice. Let me introduce you to an approach to lesson planning that has been useful in my own work. Hopefully it will provide some insight and help as you plan and prepare to teach.

Guidelines for Planning a Lesson

Before we even begin to organize the actual teaching session, there are some important first steps in planning a lesson, whether we are using a prepared lesson plan or are creating our own. These first steps include:

1. *Pray for guidance.* I believe it is important that we center all that we do in prayer. Beginning our lesson planning with prayer reminds us of who is really in charge here and helps to keep us open to the guiding of the Spirit throughout our planning and our teaching. Begin with prayer!

2. *Think about your students.* Think about the people you will be teaching. Who are they? What do you know about them in terms of age, capabilities, needs, where they are in their developmental journey, and how they learn? What might they already know about the theme you will be exploring and why would this theme matter to them? Remember: we teach students, not lessons!

3. *Think about yourself.* This is not a call to self-centeredness but a reminder that who we are influences how we teach. It is important to give some thought to your own gifts and strengths as a teacher, to the model of teacher that informs your work. We need to reflect on how we like to learn and remember that we unconsciously teach to our own learning style. If we want to help our students learn, we will need to expand our approaches and be willing to try new things. We need to think about our own feelings and thoughts about the biblical passage or the issue/theme we are teaching. What perspectives and biases do we bring with us to this lesson? How will these help or hinder our students' learning?

4. *Be familiar with the content.* A teacher needs to be familiar with what she or he is teaching. If you are using a prepared curriculum resource, you need to read and review all of the materials, including the teacher's book, the student's book (if there is one), any activity sheets, and other resources provided. If your focus is a biblical text, it is important to read it and become familiar with it, using the guidelines for Bible study offered in chapter 5. If you have chosen a topic or issue to study, make sure you are familiar with it and have studied it enough to have a grasp of it. Knowing the content is one of the core responsibilities of a teacher.

5. *Decide on your purpose and goal for the session.* Think about what you would like your students to learn. What is it you want them to know? What is the main idea you want to work with? What do you want to accomplish during the class session? It is helpful to write a statement of purpose for the lesson. Use action verbs to write this, such as *discover, discuss, hear, make, play, learn, do,* and so on. A purpose statement helps you focus the lesson clearly in your mind. It helps you answer the question, "What is this lesson all about?" Knowing where you are going with a lesson is important to both you and the students.

Outline of a Lesson Plan

Once you've taken time to pray and to think about your students, yourself, the content you are teaching, and the purpose and goal for the lesson, it is time to organize the teaching session and develop your lesson plan. There are generally five major components to a lesson plan:

1. Opening the Session

The first thing that teachers and students do in a session is one of the most important activities of the whole lesson.

It sets the tone for the rest of the lesson, helps students get started, become engaged, and begin to answer the important question, "Why should I be interested in this?" (Remember what we learned about the brain!)

Because of the importance of beginning with what our students know, I believe we need to begin our lessons with the students themselves and help them to name their present thoughts and perspectives on the text or topic being studied. What do they already know and what do they already think about this? Opening the session needs to include the students, their voices, and their perspectives.

Some ways in which a lesson might begin include:

- Students read the biblical passage aloud and, together, teacher and students make a list of the questions they have about it.
- The teacher reads the biblical passage and asks students what they hear and what caught their attention.
- The teacher and students brainstorm the meaning of a word or phrase. For example, when teaching young children Psalm 23, a teacher might ask students to think about the word *shepherd* and make a list of who they think a shepherd is and what they think a shepherd does.
- A video clip, a photo, a song, or an object that relates to the topic is presented and students invited to give responses. Using the example above, a teacher might have several pictures of shepherds and ask students to reflect on what they see.

2. Presenting Information on the Text or Topic

Before students can engage in purposeful study about the text or topic, some basic information is usually needed and must be presented in some way. Here we move from starting the lesson to developing it further. We may use many ways to present needed information. It is important to think about ways that are appropriate for your students and will help them learn.

Some ways of presenting information include:

- The teacher makes a brief presentation, tells a story, or gives a lecture.
- Students themselves research the information, using resources provided by the teacher, and make presentations to the class. For biblical texts, these resources might include Bible commentaries, dictionaries, and atlases. For a topic, they might include magazine or newspaper articles the teacher brings in.
- A guest speaker, a video or DVD, a film, or an audio recording is used. If there is computer access, the Internet might be a resource of information.

Remember—it is important that the teacher does homework regarding the biblical text or topic and has some basic knowledge from which to draw. Even if the students research it themselves, the teacher needs to be able to help them draw appropriate conclusions about the text or topic.

3. Exploring the Text or Topic

It is important that students be encouraged to move deeper into the text or topic being studied. This means that we need to think about how we move them from just having information about the text or topic to the point where they probe more deeply and begin to make connections and develop meanings for themselves. We want to move them to active knowledge. Generally this step encourages the students to be involved with and working with the material themselves.

Some ways of exploring further the material being studied include:

- Students continue to do research on the text or topic. Some examples are interviewing a knowledgeable person, searching through additional resources to find out more, talking with other class members about what they are learning, or using a teacher-prepared worksheet to explore further.
- Students participate in discussion with carefully chosen questions to guide their reflections and challenge them to probe deeper.

Questions are a key resource in this particular step of the lesson. Learning to ask the right kind of question is the key. Remember the different kinds of questions. Information questions simply ask for information: "What do you know about this topic?" Analytical questions ask us to analyze and think: "What do you think about this topic?" And integrative questions ask us about meaning: "What does this topic mean to you?" It is particularly important that we use analytical and integrative questions in order to encourage students to explore the material being studied.

4. Responding to the Text or Topic

We reach a point in the lesson where we want to help the students respond to what they are learning and to express what it is meaning to them. This step helps students to decide what they will do with what they know. Because our students learn in different ways, it is important to offer a variety of opportunities through which they can respond to what they are learning and to express their meanings in their own unique ways.

Some ways of responding to the text or topic:

- The students engage in drama or the arts to express their learnings. For example, young children are invited to create a picture that represents their understanding of

Psalm 23, or adolescents are asked to present a drama that retells a biblical story in their own words, reflecting what it means to them.

- Students decide to undertake a particular action, like taking part in a hunger walk as a response to a study of Matthew 25:31–46.
- Students write a modern-day version of a biblical text to express what it means to them today.

Students may respond in many ways to the lesson content. What is important here is to offer students ways that are useful to them and truly help them name their important learnings and insights.

5. Closing the Session

Each lesson needs to be brought to a fitting conclusion so that students and the teacher sense some completion in that particular session. Even if you have been unable to move through all of the steps outlined in this lesson plan guide, it is important to bring closure to the time together and to build a bridge to the next session. This means paying attention to time so that the bell ending class does not ring when you are in the middle of a sentence, and students start rushing for the door.

Some ways to conclude a lesson include:

- Students share their creative responses.
- Teacher and students together summarize what has been learned. This can be done simply by asking students to name an important learning they have had.
- The class prays together or shares in a brief closing worship experience.
- The teacher and students decide on a project or action that will continue the learning in the next session.

The important thing is to have opportunity to name learnings and to help students see the meanings that they are making.

At the end of your lesson planning, take time to make a list of things that need to be done, like arranging the room in a particular way, and of the materials you will need. Having these on a checklist can help you avoid that panicked feeling when you arrive in class on Sunday morning and wonder whether you have what you need.

The lesson-planning guide I have presented here is meant to be suggestive and not a rigid process you need to follow. If you are using prepared curriculum resources, thinking about these steps helps you to be sensitive to how the writer of your particular resource has attended to opening the session, to presenting information, to exploring the material, to helping students respond to what they are learning and to bringing closure to the session. All of these are important movements in the learning process. Not all of the steps will occur as distinct moments in the classroom. This is especially true with steps two, three, and four—presenting, exploring, responding—which often happen interwoven together. For example, we present information about a text or topic and at the same time ask questions that invite students to think more deeply about it. In developing their responses to what they have learned, students continue the process of probing the material for deeper insights. Remember, the goal is not to follow the steps of the process but to help our students learn!

In selecting whatever activities you choose to help you open, present, explore, respond and close the session, it is vital to remember what we've learned about the brain and how it learns. The less students simply sit and listen and the more they are actively engaged in the learning process, the greater the possibility that they will be connected with the lesson and that they will learn in ways meaningful to them.

In addition to the guidelines and outline presented above, a few final suggestions can assist you as you plan and prepare lessons. First, it is important that you not wait until Saturday night to prepare your lesson for Sunday morning. Taking time early in the week to begin to think about and prepare the lesson is invaluable. Reading through the resources and/or the text early on helps you think about the lesson throughout the week. The more you live with and think about a text, the more it becomes familiar to you and helps you make connections you can share with others. Besides, knowing on Monday that you will need to have certain supplies on hand can avoid a lot of last minute rushing around.

If you are a new teacher, don't be afraid to consult with a more experienced teacher, with your pastor or minister of Christian education, or with the Christian education committee who asked you to teach. The ministry of teaching is not a "lone ranger" activity where you have to do it all on your own. It is okay to reach out and draw on the wisdom and experience of those who can help you in understanding who you teach, what you teach, and how you teach. I encourage you to use the resources listed at the end of this chapter and to ask your church to provide some of these for you. Developing a resource center for teachers is an invaluable gift a church can offer those it has called to teach.

Summary

Planning and preparing lessons is one of the core practices of teaching. Our lessons serve as road maps and help us know where we are going and how we are going to get there. Taking time to think about our students, about ourselves as teachers and what we bring, about the material we will teach, and about the purpose and goal toward which we are working provides the starting point for lesson planning. Organizing our lessons so that we are intentional about how we open the session, how we present information, how we help our students explore the material, how we assist them in responding to what they are learning, and how we close the session is at the heart of lesson planning.

Taking the time needed to plan and prepare each week is a necessary part of this practice. Reaching out for the help we need from those who can assist in guiding us in our tasks reflects our willingness to take seriously our call to teach. Remembering always that people are at the heart of our teaching, we still acknowledge that well-planned and prepared lessons enable us to teach and lead our students in ways that can be transformative in their lives. Giving our best effort to the teaching practice of planning and preparing lessons is vital to our ministry.

Further Reflection

1. Think about a lesson you have taught. Outline that lesson, naming the steps you followed. How do these compare to the lesson plan outline in this chapter? What will you keep the same and what will you do different in your lesson plans?

2. What have you learned about lesson planning from this chapter? What additional help with planning lessons would you like? Who can provide that help?

3. Check to see which of the listed resources for lesson planning and selecting methods are available in your church. What other resources does your church provide? Encourage your church to develop a resource library for its teachers.

Resources for Lesson Planning and Selecting Teaching Methods

Blair, Christine. *The Art of Teaching the Bible.* Louisville: Geneva Press, 2001.

Bracke, John, and Karen Tye. *Teaching the Bible in the Church.* St. Louis: Chalice Press, 2003.

Bruce, Barbara. *Seven Ways of Teaching the Bible to Children.* Nashville: Abingdon Press, 1996.

Foster, Charles. *The Ministry of the Volunteer Teacher.* Nashville: Abingdon Press, 1986.

Griggs, Donald L. *Teaching Today's Teachers to Teach.* Nashville: Abingdon Press, 2003.

Halverson, Delia. *32 Ways to Become a Great Sunday School Teacher.* Nashville: Abingdon Press, 1997.

Juengst, Sara Covin. *Equipping the Saints: Teacher Training in the Church.* Louisville: Westminster John Knox Press, 1998.

LeFever, Marlene D. *Creative Teaching Methods.* Elgin, Ill.: David C. Cook, 1985.

Murray, Dick. *Teaching the Bible to Adults and Youth.* Nashville: Abingdon Press, 1987.

Smith, Judy Gattis. *Joyful Teaching–Joyful Learning.* Nashville: Discipleship Resources, 1986.

____. *Twenty-six Ways to Use Drama in Teaching the Bible.* Nashville: Abingdon Press, 1988.

Postscript

"I touch the future—I teach."[1]

It has been said that the church is only one generation away from extinction. If we are not teaching the present generations, passing on the stories and traditions and helping people know what it means to live as Christians in their daily lives, then our future looks bleak. While I do not want to end this book on a negative note, I do want to continue the challenge offered by the Ethiopian eunuch in Acts 8:26–40 when asked by the apostle Philip if he understood what he was reading in the book of Isaiah. The eunuch replied, "How can I, unless someone guides me?"

You have been called to guide others into the future of the church. My hope is that in the preceding pages you have gained insight into this vital calling and ministry of teaching. I hope you are able to see in yourself the qualities of a teacher and are open to the various roles you may be called to play. I hope you embrace the foundational practices of teaching and are committed to knowing your students, knowing your subject matter, creating an effective learning environment,

---

[1]A widely quoted saying of Christa McAuliffe, the teacher who died in the *Challenger* space shuttle explosion. As quoted in Sara Covin Juengst, *Equipping the Saints: Teacher Training in the Church* (Louisville: Westminster John Knox Press, 1998), 79.

and giving careful attention to planning and preparing the lessons you teach.

It is important work to which you have been called. But it is not all work. There is joy in teaching, too, and sometimes it comes in the small and ordinary moments of life. Joy comes in that moment in church when your eyes meet those of a child you are teaching and you see the light of recognition and a shy smile form on his face. Joy comes when you see the excitement in your students' faces as they discover a new and important learning. Joy comes when you watch an adolescent find her voice and speak out about a justice issue that concerns her. Joy comes when a student says, "I want to know more about that. Can you help me?" Joy comes when we realize that we touch the future—we teach.

Many years ago a former student sent me a card that celebrated teachers. On this card was a poem, written by an anonymous author. This poem hangs in a frame over my desk to remind me daily of the power and promise of teaching. It goes like this:

Enable me to teach with wisdom for I help to shape the mind.

Equip me to teach with truth for I help to shape the conscience.

Encourage me to teach with vision for I help to shape the future.

Empower me to teach with love for I help to shape the world.

The mind, the conscience, the future, and the world—we touch them all. Such is the responsibility and joy of teaching. May you embrace your calling as a teacher knowing that you shape the world!

Also from Karen B. Tye...

Basics of Christian Education

"Certain books belong in the library of every Christian educator. Karen Tye's *Basics of Christian Education* is one of them. With eight fundamental questions, and a discussion of the search for answers, she provides a foundation for approaching the ministry of education in the church."

The Education Connection

"True to her title, Karen Tye explores basics of Christian education, inviting readers to explore diverse perspectives and to identify and stretch their own perspectives. Writing in an accessible style with illustrative stories, Tye engages readers in dialogue from the very beginning. With simplicity and clarity, she articulates questions at the heart of educational ministry: why, where, what, who, and how. The result is a broad-ranging book that can be used to stir further dialogue in local churches, as well as seminary and college classrooms."

Mary Elizabeth Moore, Candler School of Theology

"*Basics of Christian Education* embraces the complexity and ambiguity of congregational life. Karen Tye provides practical resources and helps us engage the messiness, fears, and routines of church life in an effort to respond faithfully to God's grace."

Jack L. Seymour, Garrett-Evangelical Thological Seminary

978-08272-02290, $18.99

1-800-366-3383 • www.chalicepress.com

Also from Karen B. Tye...

Teaching the Bible in the Church
by John M. Bracke and Karen B. Tye

"Bracke and Tye have written a remarkable book, one only possible in an interdisciplinary conversation. The book works—and works well!—at the interface between 'state of the art' educational theory about the learning processes and the cruciality of biblical faith...It is an offer that warrants close study and courageous enactment, a welcome voice amid current church ferment."

Walter Brueggemann, Columbia Theological Seminary

"Teaching the Bible involves more than a simple exploration of the biblical text. Through a holistic reflection of the nature and role of teaching, learning, culture, and biblical interpretation, John Bracke and Karen Tye guide teachers through the complexities of the task of teaching the Bible. An innovative and practical resource, *Teaching the Bible in the Church* will better equip pastors, teachers, and religious educators to create teaching and learning environments that are engaging, affirming, transformative, and life giving."

Yolanda Y. Smith, Yale University Divinity School

978-08272-36431, $19.99

 **CHALICE**
PRESS

1-800-366-3383 • www.chalicepress.com

Also from the Your Calling as...*series*

Your Calling as a Christian
by Timothy L. Carson

Your Calling as a Christian is a "conversation about some of the most profound questions in life." How does one know God and truth? How is the Christian faith unique? Why should I care? Addressing such mysteries, author Tim Carson writes for those looking for a greater understanding of the Christian faith and the hope that it promises.

"If I hadn't just put down *Your Calling as a Christian,* I would have insisted that such a book was impossible to write: a book where you can both dip toes in the water and dive deep into the depths. Every book issues a 'call.' Hear the 'call' of this book about 'calling,' and you will find yourself answering 'calls' that will change your life and change the world."

Leonard Sweet, Drew University, George Fox Evangelical Seminary, author of Out of the Question... Into the Mystery

"Readers with questions about traditional Christianity will take comfort that someone else is raising them as well. Readers who want to dig deeper will find here a good foundation for their exploration."

Michael Kinnamon, Eden Theological Seminary

978-08272-44139, $9.99

CHALICE PRESS   1-800-366-3383 • www.chalicepress.com

Also from the Your Calling as…*series*

Your Calling as an Elder
by Gary Straub

New elders and veteran leaders alike
will find wisdom, biblical guidance,
and useful suggestions in Gary Straub's
examination of the crucial role of
elders in Christian Church (Disciples of
Christ) congregations.

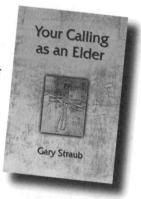

This simple and easy to read
overview of Disciples eldership
examines the nature of the office
and describes its responsibilities
and challenges. It emphasizes the
importance of spirituality in the lives
of elders.

Straub beckons elders to embark on their leadership
adventure together, fortifying their leadership through
prayer, learning, discussion, mutual accountability, and
other paths to spiritual growth and encouragement.

Their faithful eldership is a beacon for faithful
congregations as elders' prayers become spiritual channels
through which graces unfold in congregational life. That
exciting prospect lies at the heart of eldership and of
Straub's inspiring insights.

978-08272-44108, $9.99

 **CHALICE** PRESS   1-800-366-3383 • www.chalicepress.com

Also from the Your Calling as…*series*

Your Calling as a Deacon
by Gary Straub and James Trader II

"Folksy, almost breezy, language disguises serious, insightful spiritual counsel to those seeking to discover their call to diaconal ministry. This long-needed book will contribute greatly to those searching to see if they fit this lay ministry, those already serving as deacons, and those who seek to equip the ministry of the diaconate. Don't let this easily read book keep you from appreciating its depth and its praciticality."

> *Peter M. Morgan, retired president, Disciples of Christ Historical Society, author of* Disciples Eldership/A Quest for Identity and Ministry

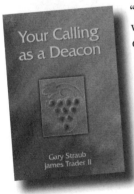

"'An adventure with God.' Is that the way the people in your congregation describe their ministry as deacons? *Your Calling as a Deacon* provides biblical understanding and insightful encouragement for all who would serve in this role. The church needs to reclaim an adventurous faith. Deacons who embody the spirit and practices of this book can lead us in that direction."

> *William B. Kincaid III, pastor, Woodland Christian Church, Lexington, Kentucky*

978-08272-44115, $9.99

 CHALICE PRESS

1-800-366-3383 • www.chalicepress.com

Also from the Your Calling as...*series*

Your Calling as a Leader
by Gary Straub and Judy G. Turner

Your Calling as a Leader calls the church to seek out and develop spiritual leaders. It is filled with real-life illustrations to help groups and individuals discern God's direction and God's design for the church even through the most difficult situations.

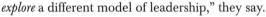

While many decry a dwindling supply of church leaders, authors Gary Straub and Judy Turner view the situation as an opportunity to grow leaders in new ways. "Let's not *deplore* the leadership crisis; let's *explore* a different model of leadership," they say.

As it focuses on principles of spiritual leadership, *Your Calling as a Leader* provides concrete applications that show congregations how to reach spiritual agreement and intentionally train spirit leaders. It calls every Christian to find the leader role God wants him or her to fill.

978-08272-44122, $9.99

 **CHALICE PRESS**   1-800-366-3383 • www.chalicepress.com